Spelling Through
Morphographs

A Direct Instruction Program

Student Workbook

Robert Dixon

Siegfried Engelmann

Columbus, OH

The McGraw·Hill Companies

Contents

Lessons

Resources

SRAonline.com

 SRA

Copyright © 2007 by SRA/McGraw-Hill.

Send all inquiries to:
SRA/McGraw-Hill
4400 Easton Commons
Columbus, OH 43219

Printed in the United States of America.

ISBN 0-07-605395-4
    978-0-07-605395-7

5 6 7 8 9 DBH 12 11 10 09 08 07

The McGraw·Hill Companies

Lesson 1

Name _____ Date _____

Part A

1. _____ ring

2. _____ ringing

3. _____ wondering

4. _____ wonder

5. _____ renting

6. _____ react

7. _____ watering

8. _____ repacking

Part B

1. _____

2. _____

3. _____

4. _____

5. _____

6. _____

Part C

1. _____   3. _____

2. _____   4. _____

Part D

1. _____ + _____ = wondering

2. _____ + _____ + _____ = repacking

3. _____ + _____ = reborn

4. _____ + _____ = spending

PART	A	B	C	D	E	F	G	Worksheet Errors	Worksheet Points	Oral Points	Bonus Points	Total Points
										+	+	=

Lesson 2

Name _____ Date _____

Part A

1. _____ resting
2. _____ rest
3. _____ string
4. _____ reborn
5. _____ quieting
6. _____ stringing
7. _____ refreshing
8. _____ watering

Part B

1. _____
2. _____
3. _____

Part C

1. _____
2. _____
3. _____
4. _____
5. _____
6. _____

Part D

1. _____
2. _____
3. _____
4. _____
5. _____
6. _____

Part E

1. _____ + _____ + _____ = relighting
2. _____ + _____ = brushing
3. _____ + _____ = refresh
4. _____ + _____ = crashing

PART	A	B	C	D	E	F	G	Worksheet Errors	Worksheet Points	Oral Points	Bonus Points	Total Points
										+	+	=

Lesson 3

Name _____ Date _____

Part A

1. _____ refresh
2. _____ resting
3. _____ rest
4. _____ rent
5. _____ refreshing
6. _____ wondering
7. _____ ringing
8. _____ ring

Part B

1. _____
2. _____
3. _____
4. _____

Part C

1. _____
2. _____
3. _____
4. _____
5. _____
6. _____
7. _____
8. _____

Part D

1. _____ + _____ = wondering
2. _____ + _____ + _____ = repacking
3. _____ + _____ = spending
4. _____ + _____ + _____ = unpacking

Part E

Circle the words in the lines.

1. (quiet) quietqueitquitequietpuietqnietquiettquiet

2. (light) ligthlightlligtlitelightlightlightllightlitgh

3. (refresh) refershrefreshrefersrefershrefrcshrefresherefresh

4. (wondering) wonduringwwonderingwonderinwonderinggwondering

PART	A	B	C	D	E	F	G	Worksheet Errors	Worksheet Points	Oral Points	Bonus Points	Total Points
										+	+	=

Lesson 4

Name _____ Date _____

Part A

1. _____ fun

2. _____ unborn

3. _____ fresh

4. _____ refreshing

Part B

Draw a line from each morphograph to its meaning.

re •

ing •

un •

• when you do something

• again

• not

Part C

1. _____

2. _____

3. _____

Part D

1. _____

2. _____

3. _____

4. _____

5. _____

6. _____

Part E

1. _____ + _____ = unpack

2. _____ + _____ = report

3. _____ + _____ + _____ = resorting

Part F

1. (thickest)   thickestthickistthicknessthickestthickestthickset

2. (unpack)   unpaekunpackununpakeunpackuunpackunpackunpack

PART	A	B	C	D	E	F	G	Worksheet Errors	Worksheet Points	Oral Points	Bonus Points	Total Points
									+	+	=	

Name _____ Date _____

Part A

1. _____   5. _____

2. _____   6. _____

3. _____   7. _____

4. _____

Part B

1. _____   3. _____

2. _____   4. _____

Part C

Draw a line from each morphograph to its meaning.

re •   • when you do something

ing •   • the most

est •   • again

un •   • not

Part D

1. _____ + _____ + _____ = reporting

2. _____ + _____ = unhappy

3. _____ + _____ = quieting

4. _____ + _____ = respell

5. _____ + _____ = lighting

6. _____ + _____ = resort

Name _____ Date _____

Part E

Circle the words in the lines.

1. (refreshing)   refresingrefershingrefreshingreefreshing

2. (light)   ligthlighttlitelightlitghlightlightlifth

3. (quietest)   quietestqueitestqueitistquietestpuietest

4. (match)   machmatchnatchmatchmmatchnatshmatshmatch

Bonus Exercise

1. **quiet**   qui __ t   qu __ __ t   q __ __ __ t   __ __ __ __ __

2. **match**   mat __ h   ma __ __ h   ma __ __ __   m __ __ __ h   __ __ __ __ __

3. **thick**   thic __   thi __ __   th __ __ __   t __ __ __ __   __ __ __ __ __

4. **brush**   br __ sh   br __ __ h   b __ __ __ h   __ __ __ __ h   __ __ __ __ __

5. **light**   lig __ t   li __ __ t   li __ __ __   l __ __ __ __   __ __ __ __ __

6. **fresh**   f __ esh   f __ __ sh   f __ __ __ h   __ __ __ __ h   __ __ __ __ __

PART	A	B	C	D	E	F	G	Worksheet Errors	Worksheet Points	Oral Points	Bonus Points	Total Points
										+	+	=

Lesson 6

Name _____ Date _____

Part A

1. _____ 3. _____

2. _____ 4. _____

Part B

1. _____ 5. _____

2. _____ 6. _____

3. _____ 7. _____

4. _____ 8. _____

Part C

1. _____ 4. _____

2. _____ 5. _____

3. _____ 6. _____

Part D

Draw a line from each morphograph to its meaning.

est •   • when you do something

re •   • without

un •   • the most

ing •   • again

less •   • not

Name _____ Date _____

Part E

1. _____ + _____ = helpless
2. _____ + _____ + _____ = unpacking
3. _____ + _____ = motoring
4. _____ + _____ = matchless
5. _____ + _____ + _____ = resorting

Part F

Circle the words in the lines.

1. (author)   autherauthorathorautherauthorauauthoranther

2. (matchless)   matchlesmatchlessmacthlessmatchlessmatcmatchless

3. (motor)   motormotromotermotorrmotormoturmctormotor

4. (brush)   drushburshbruchbrushbrurshdrushbrushbrbrush

Bonus Exercise

1. **author** auth __ r   aut __ __ __   au __ __ __ __   a __ __ __ __ __ __   __ __ __ __ __ __

2. **light**   l __ ght   l __ __ ht   l __ __ __ t   l __ __ __ __   __ __ __ __ __

3. **spend**   sp __ nd   sp __ __ d   s __ __ __ d   __ __ __ __ d   __ __ __ __ __

4. **quiet**   qui __ t   qu __ __ t   q __ __ __ t   __ __ __ __ t   __ __ __ __ __

5. **wonder** won __ __ r   w __ n __ __ __   w __ __ __ __ __   __ __ __ __ __ __

6. **motor**   m __ tor   m __ __ or   m __ __ __ r   __ __ __ __ r   __ __ __ __ __

PART	A	B	C	D	E	F	G	Worksheet Errors	Worksheet Points	Oral Points	Bonus Points	Total Points
										+	+	=

Name _____ Date _____

Part A

1. _____ 3. _____

2. _____ 4. _____

Part B

b   u   h   o   t   e   i   n   c

Part C

1. _____ 3. _____

2. _____ 4. _____

Part D

Figure out each word and write it in the blank below.

huanppy   aothru

1. _____ 2. _____

amcht   rerefsh

3. _____ 4. _____

Part E

Draw a line from each morphograph to its meaning.

mis •   • not

re •   • again

less •   • wrongly

un •   • without

Part F

Fill in the blanks to show the morphographs in each word.

1. _____ + _____ + _____ = misspending

2. _____ + _____ = grandest

3. _____ + _____ = matchless

4. _____ + _____ + _____ = refreshing

PART	A	B	C	D	E	F	G	Worksheet Errors	Worksheet Points	Oral Points	Bonus Points	Total Points
										+	+	=

Lesson 8

Name _____ Date _____

Part A

1. _____ 3. _____

2. _____ 4. _____

Part B

n   e   c   j   k   o   v   d   l

p   a   r   f   u   e   i   o   t

Part C

1. _____ 4. _____

2. _____ 5. _____

3. _____ 6. _____

Part D

Figure out each word and write it in the blank below.

endfri   mssiepll   shestfre

1. _____ 2. _____ 3. _____

wingdoner   mastike

4. _____ 5. _____

Part E

Fill in the blanks to show the morphographs in each word.

1. _____ + _____ = unhuman

2. _____ + _____ = stretching

3. _____ + _____ + _____ = unfilling

4. _____ + _____ + _____ = mismatching

5. _____ + _____ = thickest

6. _____ + _____ = helpless

Name _____ Date _____

Part F

Draw a line from each morphograph to its meaning.

mis •   • not

est •   • again

ing •   • the most

un •   • without

less •   • wrongly

re •   • when you do something

Part G

Circle the words in the lines.

1. (stretch)   stretchstretchstrecthstretchstertchstretchststretch

2. (human)   humenhumanhnuanhumanhuhumannnumanhumanhumahhuman

3. (friend)   freindfriendffriendfirendfriendfrendfriendfrienfriend

4. (authoring)   authorauthoringautheringsauthoringangauthoring

PART	A	B	C	D	E	F	G	Worksheet Errors	Worksheet Points	Oral Points	Bonus Points	Total Points
										+	+	=

Lesson 9

Name _____ Date _____

Part A

1. _____ 2. _____

Part B

1. _____ 4. _____

2. _____ 5. _____

3. _____

Part C

b   e   i   r   t   u   l   o   p

a   c   v   n   i   k   j   t   u

Part D

1. _____ 3. _____

2. _____ 4. _____

Part E

Figure out each word and write it in the blank below.

sterhct   ingcrsha   othuar

1. _____ 2. _____ 3. _____

munha   fienrd   lghitste

4. _____ 5. _____ 6. _____

Name _____ Date _____

Part F

Draw a line from each morphograph to its meaning.

un •   • when you do something

mis •   • that which is

ing •   • not

less •   • without

est •   • wrongly

re •   • the most

ness •   • again

Part G

Circle the words in the lines.

1. (pressing)   pressignpressingpresspressingperssingpressingingpress

2. (unpack)   unpaeknupackunupackunpacknubackunbackunpackpack

3. (stretch)   stertchstretchsrstrcthstretcstretcnstretchstertch

4. (lightest)   litghestlightlightistlightestligthestlightestlilightesl

PART	A	B	C	D	E	F	G	Worksheet Errors	Worksheet Points	Oral Points	Bonus Points	Total Points
										+	+	=

Name _____ Date _____

Part A

1. _____   5. _____

2. _____   6. _____

3. _____   7. _____

4. _____   8. _____

Part B

a   c   i   m   s   u   d   o   p

v   e   o   u   n   t   z   r   k

Part C

1. _____   3. _____

2. _____   4. _____

Part D

Write each of these words in a box. Write "free space" in one box.

stretch	thickest	misspelling	report	helpless
unhappy	dullest	dullness	friendly	define
author	matchless	crashing	right	catcher

PART	A	B	C	D	E	F	G	Worksheet Errors	Worksheet Points	Oral Points	Bonus Points	Total Points
										+	+	=

Lesson 11

Name _____ Date _____

Part A

1. _____ 5. _____

2. _____ 6. _____

3. _____ 7. _____

4. _____

Part B

Write each of these words in a box. Write "free space" in one box.

stretching	refreshing	helpless	quietness	mismatch
take	misspend	brushing	backless	freshness
refillable	repacking	unborn	thickness	motor

Part C

b r e n o p z

i a g u k i e

Part D

Figure out each word and write it in the blank below.

heplnseslses   preress   itstrcheng

1. _____ 2. _____ 3. _____

drienf   kate   smellisp

4. _____ 5. _____ 6. _____

Name _____ Date _____

Part E

Draw a line from each morphograph to its meaning.

un •   • again

est •   • when you do something

ness •   • not

less •   • can be

re •   • the most

ing •   • wrongly

able •   • that which is

mis •   • without

Part F

Circle the words in the lines.

1. (author)   anthorauthauthorrauthorauothorauthoraautnorauthor

2. (mismatch)   mismatcmismatshmismatchmismatmismatchmismacth

3. (quietest)   queitestquietistquietquietestqnietestquietest

4. (misspell)   mispelllmisspelmisspellmisspelmispelmisspellmispel

Bonus Exercise

1. **stretch**   str _ tch   st _ _ tch   st _ _ _ ch   s _ _ _ _ _ _   _ _ _ _ _ _ _

2. **quiet**   qui _ t   qu _ _ t   q _ _ _ t   _ _ _ _ t   _ _ _ _ _ _

3. **thick**   th _ ck   th _ _ k   t _ _ _ k   t _ _ _ _ _   _ _ _ _ _ _

PART	A	B	C	D	E	F	G	Worksheet Errors	Worksheet Points	Oral Points	Bonus Points	Total Points
										+	+	=

Lesson 12

Name _____ Date _____

Part A

1. Kit was _____ about the _____ .

2. I'm going to _____ out and enjoy a good tennis _____ .

Part B

1. _____   3. _____

2. _____

Part C

Write the word for each meaning.

	word	meaning
1.	_____	that which is thick
2.	_____	can be stretched
3.	_____	when you press
4.	_____	spell wrongly
5.	_____	not born
6.	_____	the most grand
7.	_____	without help

Part D

Make a little v above every vowel letter. Make a little c above every consonant letter.

u   b   n   i   o   k   l

a   e   q   t   i   h   a

Name _____ Date _____

Part E

Draw a line from each morphograph to its meaning.

able •   • without

ness •   • can be

ing •   • that which is

less •   • when you do something

Part F

Figure out each word and write it in the blank below.

ssepr   fnierd

1. _____   2. _____

serort   ghtil

3. _____   4. _____

Part G

Circle the words in each line.

1. (portable)   portalbeportableprotableportebleportablepoportalbe

2. (misspend)   mispendmisspnedmissspendmismisspendmissendmisspend

3. (author)   authorautheranthorauthauthorawthosauthoraauthor

4. (humanness)   humanesshumannesshumaneshunamnesshumannesshumaness

PART	A	B	C	D	E	F	G	Worksheet Errors	Worksheet Points	Oral Points	Bonus Points	Total Points
									+	+	=	

Lesson 14

Name _____ Date _____

Part A

1. _____   3. _____

2. _____   4. _____

Part B

1. The _____ being was not _____ .

2. An _____ and his _____ are _____ on crime.

Part C

Write the word for each meaning.

	word	meaning
1.	_____	name again
2.	_____	that which is grand
3.	_____	can be stretched
4.	_____	not like

Part D

Figure out each word and write it in the blank below.

drewon   tchestr   ifne

1. _____   2. _____   3. _____

Bonus Exercise

1. **human**   hum __ n   hu __ __ n   h __ __ __ n   __ __ __ __ n   __ __ __ __ __

2. **author**   a __ thor   a __ __ __ or   a __ __ __ __ r   __ __ __ __ __ __

PART	A	B	C	D	E	F	G	Worksheet Errors	Worksheet Points	Oral Points	Bonus Points	Total Points
										+	+	=

Lesson 15

Name _____ Date _____

Part A

1. _____   4. _____

2. _____   5. _____

3. _____   6. _____

Part B

1. like + able   = _____   6. human + ness = _____

2. match + less   = _____   7. use + able   = _____

3. like + ness   = _____   8. use + ful   = _____

4. help + ing   = _____   9. wide + est   = _____

5. dine + ing   = _____   10. face + ing   = _____

Part C

1. _____   3. _____

2. _____   4. _____

Part D

Draw a line from each morphograph to its meaning.

un •   • without

est •   • not

ness •   • that which is

less •   • again

re •   • the most

Part E

Write the word for each meaning.

word	meaning
1. _____	help in the past
2. _____	fill again
3. _____	spell wrongly
4. _____	the most grand
5. _____	without hope

PART	A	B	C	D	E	F	G	Worksheet Errors	Worksheet Points	Oral Points	Bonus Points	Total Points
									+	+	=	

Lesson 16

Name _____ Date _____

Part A

1. _____   4. _____

2. _____   5. _____

3. _____

Part B

1. use + less   = _____   7. bare + ness   = _____

2. friend + less   = _____   8. note + able   = _____

3. care + ing   = _____   9. note + ing   = _____

4. stretch + able = _____   10. author + ing = _____

5. dine + ed   = _____   11. take + ing   = _____

6. quiet + ed   = _____   12. care + less   = _____

Part C

Write each of these words in a box. Write "free space" in one box.

grade	quietness	use	wide	wondered
refine	night	hope	lightest	thickest
misspelling	right	humanness	dullness	stretchable

Name _____ Date _____

Part D

Figure out each word and write it in the blank below.

ghtir   rothau   lefirl

1. _____ 2. _____ 3. _____

Part E

Circle the words in the lines.

1. (night)   nightrightnigthinighthginightniphtnight

2. (stretching)   stretchingstretchingstrecthingstretchingstretching

3. (use)   uzeuseususeuuseaseuseseuseyouuse

Bonus Exercise

1. **right**   ri __ ht   r __ __ ht   r __ __ __ t   __ __ __ __ t   __ __ __ __ __

2. **serve**   serv __   ser __ __   se __ __ __   s __ __ __ __   __ __ __ __ __

3. **hope**   ho __ e   h __ __ e   h __ __ __   __ __ __ e   __ __ __ __

4. **human**   h __ man   h __ __ an   h __ __ __ n   __ __ __ __ n   __ __ __ __ __

PART	A	B	C	D	E	F	G	Worksheet Errors	Worksheet Points	Oral Points	Bonus Points	Total Points
									+	+	=	

Lesson 17

Name _____ Date _____

Part A

1. _____ 4. _____

2. _____ 5. _____

3. _____ 6. _____

Part B

1. dine + ing   = _____   8. name + less   = _____

2. wide + ness   = _____   9. name + ing   = _____

3. catch + able = _____   10. like + able   = _____

4. serve + ing   = _____   11. like + ness   = _____

5. trace + ing   = _____   12. dull + est   = _____

6. motor + ing   = _____   13. dull + ness   = _____

7. bare + ed   = _____   14. care + ing   = _____

Part C

1. _____

2. _____

3. _____

4. _____

5. _____

6. _____

Part D

Draw a line from each morphograph to its meaning.

re   •   • not

ing   •   • again

un   •   • without

est   •   • when you do something

less •   • the most

PART	A	B	C	D	E	F	G	Worksheet Errors	Worksheet Points	Oral Points	Bonus Points	Total Points
										+	+	=

Name _____ Date _____

Part A

1. Toronto is a large and beautiful _____ .

2. Before the tennis _____ , we did _____ exercises.

3. Janie _____ a marble from her _____ .

4. The waiter will _____ a _____ lunch.

5. Our _____ during the holiday was pure _____ .

Part B

1. snap   3. sad   5. wander   7. sell
2. face   4. shop   6. catch   8. mad

Part C

1. _____ + _____ = _____
2. _____ + _____ = _____
3. _____ + _____ = _____
4. _____ + _____ = _____
5. _____ + _____ = _____
6. _____ + _____ = _____
7. _____ + _____ = _____
8. _____ + _____ = _____

Name _____ Date _____

Part D

These words are in the puzzle.
Circle 7 or more of the words.

author	human	sad
thick	grand	name
lock	handed	ate
stretch	wide	help

```
h a t l w i d e
a u t h o r r h
n a m e i c c e
d k s a d c k l
e g r a n d k p
d s t r e t c h
```

Part E

Write the word for each meaning.

	word	meaning
1.	_____	one who helps
2.	_____	pack before
3.	_____	fill in the past
4.	_____	more fresh
5.	_____	stretch before
6.	_____	that which is grand
7.	_____	use wrongly
8.	_____	when you stretch

Part F

Circle the words in the lines.

1. (serve)   servesrveservesserveseverservesreve

2. (trace)   tracetratracetrasetarcetracettraceetrace

PART	A	B	C	D	E	F	G	Worksheet Errors	Worksheet Points	Oral Points	Bonus Points	Total Points
										+	+	=

Lesson 19

Name _____ Date _____

Part A

1. _____   4. _____
2. _____   5. _____
3. _____   6. _____

Part B

1. swim   4. step   7. motor
2. grade   5. arm   8. thick
3. water   6. shop   9. plan

Part C

1. _____ + _____ = _____
2. _____ + _____ = _____
3. _____ + _____ = _____
4. _____ + _____ = _____
5. _____ + _____ = _____
6. _____ + _____ = _____

Part D

These words are in the puzzle.
Circle 7 or more of the words.

right   night   light
late   than   trace
like   friend   that
note   author   grade

```
t  r  n  t  g  h  t
r  l  i  g  h  t  n
a  i  g  g  t  a  o
c  k  h  r  h  t  t
e  e  t  l  a  t  e
f  r  i  e  n  d  e
a  u  t  h  o  r  e
```

Name _____ Date _____

Part E

Draw a line from each morphograph to its meaning.

pre • • that which is

ed • • can be

er • • without

able • • one who; more

ness • • the most

less • • in the past

est • • again

re • • before

Part F

Figure out each word and write it in the blank below.

    inght   entc   dagre

1. _____ 2. _____ 3. _____

Bonus Exercise

1. **right**   r __ ght   r __ __ ht   r __ __ __ t   __ __ __ __ t   __ __ __ __ __

2. **serve**   serv __   ser __ __   se __ __ __   s __ __ __ __   __ __ __ __ __

3. **human**   hum __ n   hu __ __ n   h __ __ __ n   __ __ __ __ n   __ __ __ __ __

4. **friend**   frien __   frie __ __   fri __ __ __   fr __ __ __ __   __ __ __ __ __ __

5. **match**   m __ tch   m __ __ ch   m __ __ __ h   __ __ __ __ h   __ __ __ __ __

6. **quiet**   qu __ et   qu __ __ t   q __ __ __ t   q __ __ __ __   __ __ __ __ __

PART	A	B	C	D	E	F	G	Worksheet Errors	Worksheet Points	Oral Points	Bonus Points	Total Points
										+	+	=

Lesson 20

Name _____ Date _____

Part A

1. _____   4. _____
2. _____   5. _____
3. _____   6. _____

Part B

1. _____   5. _____
2. _____   6. _____
3. _____   7. _____
4. _____   8. _____

Part C

1. _____ + _____ = _____
2. _____ + _____ = _____
3. _____ + _____ = _____
4. _____ + _____ = _____
5. _____ + _____ = _____
6. _____ + _____ = _____
7. _____ + _____ = _____
8. _____ + _____ = _____

Part D

Look at the last three letters of each word. Make a **v** or **c** above each of the last three letters. Circle each short word that ends **cvc**. Remember, short words have four letters or fewer.

1. pen   4. wrap   7. drop
2. press   5. brother   8. brush
3. red   6. wide   9. stop

Name _____ Date _____

Part E

These words are in the puzzle.
Circle 7 or more of the words.

spell   fresh   light

friend   real   spend

seed   wide   said

name   grade   lone

```
n s p e l l
s a p f l l
f w m e o g
f r i e n d
s e e d e d
l a i s e l
l l i g h t
g r a d e t
```

Part F

Draw a line from each morphograph to its meaning.

ly •   • more; one who

er •   • before

pre •   • that which is

ed •   • not

un •   • when you do something

ness •   • in the past

ing •   • how something is done

PART	A	B	C	D	E	F	G	Worksheet Errors	Worksheet Points	Oral Points	Bonus Points	Total Points
										+	+	=

Lesson 21

Part A

1. If your answers are _____ , you'll get a good _____ .

2. The _____ sold his goods in the _____ .

3. Martin _____ _____ portions of ice cream to his guests.

4. My _____ became tired from _____ out that _____ .

5. Our ship will sail into _____ at noon.

Part B

1. _____   5. _____

2. _____   6. _____

3. _____   7. _____

4. _____

Part C

Add these morphographs together. Some of the words follow the rule about dropping the final e.

1. like + ness   = _____   9. use + ed   = _____

2. fine + est   = _____   10. dine + ing   = _____

3. name + ly   = _____   11. serve + ed   = _____

4. note + ing   = _____   12. care + less = _____

5. note + able   = _____   13. bare + ed   = _____

6. grade + ing   = _____   14. trace + ing = _____

7. wide + er   = _____   15. face + less = _____

8. hope + ing   = _____   16. hate + ing   = _____

Name _____ Date _____

Part D

Look at the last three letters of each word. Make a **v** or **c** above each of the last three letters. Circle each short word that ends **cvc**. Remember, short words have four letters or fewer.

1. plan
2. rest
3. arm
4. big
5. step
6. brother
7. clan
8. drop

Part E

Draw a line from each morphograph to its meaning.

ed •   • not

pre •   • before

er •   • without

ly •   • in the past

ness •   • when you do something

ing •   • more; one who

un •   • the most

less •   • that which is

est •   • how something is done

PART	A	B	C	D	E	F	G	Worksheet Errors	Worksheet Points	Oral Points	Bonus Points	Total Points
									+	+	=	

Lesson 22

Name _____ Date _____

Part A

Add these morphographs together. Some of the words follow the rule about dropping the final **e.**

1. note + able = _____
2. like + ing = _____
3. fine + er = _____
4. fine + ness = _____
5. fine + ly = _____
6. hope + less = _____
7. use + less = _____
8. use + ing = _____
9. trace + ing = _____
10. bare + ly = _____
11. wide + ness = _____
12. wide + ly = _____
13. wide + est = _____
14. serve + ing = _____
15. like + able = _____

Part B

Fill in the blanks to show the morphographs in each word.

1. _____ + _____ + _____ = helplessness
2. _____ + _____ = reserve
3. _____ + _____ = humanness
4. _____ + _____ = quietly
5. _____ + _____ + _____ = resorting
6. _____ + _____ = formless
7. _____ + _____ = friendly
8. _____ + _____ = stretcher
9. _____ + _____ + _____ = unpacked
10. _____ + _____ + _____ = unmatchable

Name _____ Date _____

Part C

Write the word for each meaning.

	word	**meaning**
1.	_____	that which is thick
2.	_____	press before
3.	_____	can spend
4.	_____	name wrongly
5.	_____	stretch in the past
6.	_____	without a friend
7.	_____	not happy
8.	_____	the most fresh

Part D

These words are in the puzzle.
Circle 7 or more of the words.

speller   serve   spend

city   press   part

hear   deal   care

rake   have   grade

```
s  s  s  d  p  s  g
s  p  p  e  a  h  r
p  h  e  a  r  a  a
c  c  n  l  t  v  d
i  a  d  l  l  e  e
t  r  r  a  k  e  e
y  p  r  e  s  s  r
```

PART	A	B	C	D	E	F	G	Worksheet Errors	Worksheet Points	Oral Points	Bonus Points	Total Points
										+	+	=

Lesson 24

Part A

1. _____ 4. _____

2. _____ 5. _____

3. _____ 6. _____

Part B

1. _____ + _____ = tracing

2. _____ + _____ = careless

3. _____ + _____ = faced

4. _____ + _____ = notable

5. _____ + _____ = named

6. _____ + _____ = barely

Part C

Add these morphographs together. Some of the words follow the rule about dropping the final e.

1. care + ing   = _____ 5. un + friend + ly = _____

2. cart + ed   = _____ 6. bare + ly   = _____

3. hate + ing   = _____ 7. note + able   = _____

4. mis + take + ing = _____ 8. wide + ly   = _____

Name _____ Date _____

Part D

Draw a line from each morphograph to its meaning.

ness •   • one who; more

ly •   • that which is

un •   • how something is done

able •   • not

mis •   • can be

est •   • wrongly

re •   • the most

er •   • again

Part E

Figure out each word and write it in the blank below.

lequa

1. _____

ticy

2. _____

rvesse

3. _____

PART	A	B	C	D	E	F	G	Worksheet Errors	Worksheet Points	Oral Points	Bonus Points	Total Points
										+	+	=

Lesson 25

Name _____ Date _____

Part A

Double the final **c** in a short word when the word ends **cvc** and the next morphograph begins with **v.**

1. _____   4. _____

2. _____   5. _____

3. _____

Part B

1. run + er   = _____   5. swim + ing   = _____

2. water + ed   = _____   6. mad + ly   = _____

3. sad + ness   = _____   7. form + less = _____

4. help + ful   = _____   8. sad + er   = _____

Part C

Write the word for each meaning.

word	meaning
1. _____	full of help
2. _____	away from the port
3. _____	how something is done in an equal way
4. _____	one who helps
5. _____	more fresh
6. _____	wash before
7. _____	that which is grand
8. _____	when you stretch

Name _____ Date _____

Part D

Add these morphographs together. Some of the words follow the rule about dropping the final **e.**

1. face + less   = _____

2. de + note + ing   = _____

3. mis + use + ing   = _____

4. re + fine + able   = _____

5. pre + serve + ing   = _____

6. force + ful   = _____

7. choice + est   = _____

8. care + less   = _____

Part E

Fill in the blanks to show the morphographs in each word.

1. _____ + _____ = serving

2. _____ + _____ = diner

3. _____ + _____ = wideness

4. _____ + _____ = hoping

5. _____ + _____ = hopeless

6. _____ + _____ = useful

PART	A	B	C	D	E	F	G	Worksheet Errors	Worksheet Points	Oral Points	Bonus Points	Total Points
										+	+	=

Lesson 26

Name _____ Date _____

Part A

Double the final **c** in a short word when the word ends **cvc** and the next morphograph begins with **v.**

1. I _____ to _____ in mountain lakes.

2. The _____ of this book rewrote every _____ .

3. A shark is _____ against the side of its _____ .

4. Maria was _____ because she had to _____ a picture.

5. Pierre's _____ _____ when he was twelve years old.

Part B

1. bar + ed	= _____	6. wander + ed	= _____
2. arm + ing	= _____	7. pack + ing	= _____
3. snap + ing	= _____	8. wash + able	= _____
4. mad + ness	= _____	9. shop + ing	= _____
5. plan + ed	= _____	10. run + er	= _____

Part C

1. _____   4. _____

2. _____   5. _____

3. _____   6. _____

Part D

1. _____ + _____ = _____

2. _____ + _____ = _____

3. _____ + _____ = _____

4. _____ + _____ = _____

5. _____ + _____ = _____

6. _____ + _____ = _____

7. _____ + _____ = _____

Name _____ Date _____

Part E

Draw a line from each morphograph to its meaning.

ful •   • away from

de •   • without

est •   • can be

ly •   • full of

ness •   • the most

er •   • again

pre •   • how something is done

re •   • before

less •   • more; one who

able •   • that which is

Part F

These words are in the puzzle.
Circle 7 or more of the words.

change   voice   cage

knee   choice   sink

hope   cape   force

shop   bar   sad

```
c v v v b s f
h c s o o a o
s h h c i d r
s o o a i c c
h i i p n a e
o c n e e g e
p e p k n e e
```

PART	A	B	C	D	E	F	G	Worksheet Errors	Worksheet Points	Oral Points	Bonus Points	Total Points
										+	+	=

Lesson 27

Name _____ Date _____

Part A

Double the final **c** in a short word when the word ends **cvc** and the next morphograph begins with **v.**

1. _____   4. _____

2. _____   5. _____

3. _____   6. _____

Part B

1. stop + ing   = _____   6. bliss + ful   = _____

2. bar + ing   = _____   7. snap + ing   = _____

3. form + er   = _____   8. arm + less   = _____

4. sad + ness   = _____   9. brother + ly = _____

5. plan + ed   = _____   10. sad + en   = _____

Part C

1. serve

   happy

   catcher

   frend

   _____

2. quiet

   equil

   thickness

   light

   _____

3. graid

   change

   watering

   preserve

   _____

4. human

   author

   strech

   trace

   _____

5. brush

   liht

   farm

   force

   _____

6. choise

   rage

   unhappy

   refreshing

   _____

Name _____ Date _____

Part D

Write the word for each meaning.

	word	meaning
1.	_____	to make light
2.	_____	full of hope
3.	_____	press away from
4.	_____	without hope

Part E

Add these morphographs together. Some of the words follow the rule about dropping the final **e**.

1. de + face + ing   = _____

2. change + ing   = _____

3. help + ful + ness   = _____

4. care + ful + ly   = _____

5. re + serve + ing   = _____

6. note + able   = _____

Part F

Fill in the blanks to show the morphographs in each word.

1. _____ + _____ + _____ = reserving

2. _____ + _____ + _____ = reported

3. _____ + _____ + _____ = forcefully

4. _____ + _____ + _____ = restlessness

5. _____ + _____ = blissful

PART	A	B	C	D	E	F	G	Worksheet Errors	Worksheet Points	Oral Points	Bonus Points	Total Points
										+	+	=

Lesson 28

Name _____ Date _____

Part A

1. _____ 4. _____

2. _____ 5. _____

3. _____ 6. _____

Part B

1. stop + ing   = _____ 6. mad + ness   = _____

2. shop + less   = _____ 7. bar + ed   = _____

3. shop + ing   = _____ 8. sad + ly   = _____

4. sell + er   = _____ 9. wander + ed = _____

5. swim + er   = _____ 10. quiet + ly = _____

Part C

1. face
   rename
   trase
   friendly

   _____

2. awthor
   freshness
   equal
   motor

   _____

3. spelling
   stretch
   author
   happey

   _____

4. change
   sirve
   trace
   resort

   _____

5. bliss
   force
   preserve
   moter

   _____

6. page
   chanje
   stretcher
   match

   _____

Name _____ Date _____

Part D

Draw a line from each morphograph to its meaning.

ness •   • away from

en •   • to make

ful •   • how something is done

de •   • full of

ly •   • that which is

Part E

Add these morphographs together. Some of the words follow the rule about dropping the final **e.**

1. take + en   = _____

2. rage + ed   = _____

3. re + coil + ing   = _____

4. un + change + ed = _____

5. pre + plan   = _____

Part F

Fill in the blanks to show the morphographs in each word.

1. _____ + _____ = really

2. _____ + _____ = passage

3. _____ + _____ = passing

4. _____ + _____ + _____ = unarmed

5. _____ + _____ + _____ = unchanged

6. _____ + _____ + _____ = hopefully

PART	A	B	C	D	E	F	G	Worksheet Errors	Worksheet Points	Oral Points	Bonus Points	Total Points
										+	+	=

Lesson 29

Name _____ Date _____

Part A

1. _____ 4. _____

2. _____ 5. _____

3. _____ 6. _____

Part B

Add these morphographs together. Some of the words follow the rule about doubling the final **c** in short words.

1. stop + ed   = _____   6. grand + ly   = _____

2. cart + ing   = _____   7. sad + en   = _____

3. hot + ly   = _____   8. mad + ness   = _____

4. plan + er   = _____   9. arm + ing   = _____

5. hot + est   = _____   10. big + er   = _____

Part C

Make 11 real words from the morphographs in the box.

less	care	rest	ed	ful	ing	hope

1. _____ 7. _____

2. _____ 8. _____

3. _____ 9. _____

4. _____ 10. _____

5. _____ 11. _____

6. _____

Name _____ Date _____

Part D

These words are in the puzzle.
Circle 7 or more of the words.

strength	stretch	swim
hate	rest	mash
sack	rent	best
wash	hot	catch

```
s  h  o  t  m  s  b  c
s  t  r  c  h  a  e  h
w  a  r  e  s  t  s  t
s  t  r  e  n  g  t  h
w  a  s  h  t  t  s  a
i  i  c  a  t  c  h  t
m  m  i  k  s  s  h  e
```

Part E

Circle the words in the lines.

1. (strength)   strengthstregthstrengthstrenghstrength
2. (stretch)   stretchstretchstrechstretchhstretch

Part F

1. **change**   cha __ ge   cha __ __ e   ch __ __ __ __   __ __ __ __ __ __

2. **choice**   ch __ __ ce   __ __ __ __ ce   __ __ __ __ __ e   __ __ __ __ __ __

3. **equal**   equ __ l   equ __ __   eq __ __ __   e __ __ __ __   __ __ __ __ __

PART	A	B	C	D	E	F	G	Worksheet Errors	Worksheet Points	Oral Points	Bonus Points	Total Points
										+	+	=

Lesson 30

Name _____ Date _____

Part A

1. _____   4. _____

2. _____   5. _____

3. _____

Part B

Make 10 real words from the morphographs in the box.

like	able	ing	stretch	note	ed	use

1. _____   6. _____

2. _____   7. _____

3. _____   8. _____

4. _____   9. _____

5. _____   10. _____

Part C

1. _____   4. _____

2. _____   5. _____

3. _____   6. _____

Part D

Add these morphographs together. Some of the words follow the rule about doubling the final **c** in a short word.

1. water + ing = _____   6. want + ed   = _____

2. big + est   = _____   7. sad + est   = _____

3. run + er   = _____   8. dull + ness = _____

4. sad + ly   = _____   9. snap + ing = _____

5. farm + ing   = _____   10. plan + ed = _____

Name _____ Date _____

Part E

Circle the misspelled word in each group.
Then write it correctly in the blank.

1. stretch

   strength

   wandor

   force

   _____

2. length

   choyce

   change

   equal

   _____

3. human

   stregth

   trace

   bliss

   _____

Bonus Exercise

1. **strength** stre __ gth stre __ __ th stre __ __ __ __ __ __ __ __ __ __ __ __ __

2. **stretch** str __ tch str __ __ ch str __ __ __ __ __ __ __ __ __ __

3. **wander** w __ nder w __ __ der w __ __ __ __ r __ __ __ __ __ __

4. **length** le __ gth le __ __ th l __ __ __ th __ __ __ __ __ th __ __ __ __ __ __

PART	A	B	C	D	E	F	G	Worksheet Errors	Worksheet Points	Oral Points	Bonus Points	Total Points
										+	+	=

Lesson 31

Name _____ Date _____

Part A

1. _____ + _____ = _____
2. _____ + _____ = _____
3. _____ + _____ = _____
4. _____ + _____ = _____
5. _____ + _____ = _____
6. _____ + _____ = _____

Part B

Make 11 real words from the morphographs in the box.

fine	wide	ly	est	bare	quiet	ness

1. _____   7. _____
2. _____   8. _____
3. _____   9. _____
4. _____   10. _____
5. _____   11. _____
6. _____

Part C

Write the word for each meaning.

	word	meaning
1.	_____	to make dark
2.	_____	that which is dark
3.	_____	the most dark
4.	_____	away from the port
5.	_____	without help
6.	_____	full of help

Name _____ Date _____

Part D

Draw a line from each morphograph to its meaning.

ly •   • can be

pre •   • more; one who

er •   • to make

ed •   • how something is done

able •   • before

en •   • in the past

Part E

Look at the last three letters of each word. Make a **v** or **c** above each of the last three letters. Circle each short word that ends **cvc.**

1. hot   3. clan   5. world   7. fill

2. author   4. sign   6. swim   8. snap

Part F

Fill in the blanks to show the morphographs in each word.

1. _____ + _____ = used

2. _____ + _____ + _____ = strengthening

3. _____ + _____ + _____ = prestretched

4. _____ + _____ = hoping

5. _____ + _____ + _____ = unchanged

6. _____ + _____ = shining

PART	A	B	C	D	E	F	G	Worksheet Errors	Worksheet Points	Oral Points	Bonus Points	Total Points
										+	+	=

Lesson 32

Name _____ Date _____

Part A

1. _____   4. _____

2. _____   5. _____

3. _____

Part B

1. _____ + _____ = _____

2. _____ + _____ = _____

3. _____ + _____ = _____

4. _____ + _____ = _____

5. _____ + _____ = _____

6. _____ + _____ = _____

7. _____ + _____ = _____

8. _____ + _____ = _____

Part C

Fill in the blanks to show the morphographs in each word.

1. _____ + _____ = lonely

2. _____ + _____ = swimmer

3. _____ + _____ = noted

4. _____ + _____ = grading

5. _____ + _____ = snapper

6. _____ + _____ = madness

Name _____ Date _____

Part D

Make 13 real words from the morphographs in the box.

like	wide	en	ing	ness	length	take	ly

1. _____   8. _____

2. _____   9. _____

3. _____   10. _____

4. _____   11. _____

5. _____   12. _____

6. _____   13. _____

7. _____

Part E

Circle the misspelled word in each group.
Then write it correctly in the blank.

1. forse
   serve
   stretch
   human

2. trace
   change
   voise
   length

3. friend
   auther
   real
   wander

4. grade
   night
   strength
   civel

_____   _____   _____   _____

PART	A	B	C	D	E	F	G	Worksheet Errors	Worksheet Points	Oral Points	Bonus Points	Total Points
									+	+	=	

Name _____ Date _____

Part A

1. Mr. Nelson _____ the _____ over his _____ .

2. One _____ is _____ for a _____ storm.

Part B

Write each of these words in a box. Write "free space" in one box.

equal	play	night	dropper	blissful	unchanged	stretch	wander
voice	berry	length	tracing	nerve	civil	humanly	

Part C

Add these morphographs together. Some of the words follow the rule about dropping the final e.

1. rage + ing = _____
2. race + er = _____
3. force + ful = _____
4. herb + al = _____
5. lose + er = _____
6. like + en = _____

Part D

Add these morphographs together. Some of the words follow the rule about doubling the final c in a short word.

1. sad + ness = _____
2. run + less = _____
3. big + est = _____
4. snap + less = _____

PART	A	B	C	D	E	F	G	Worksheet Errors	Worksheet Points	Oral Points	Bonus Points	Total Points
										+	+	=

Lesson 35

Name _____ Date _____

Part A

1. _____

_____

2. _____

_____

Part B

Add these morphographs together. Some of the words follow the rule about doubling the final **c** in short words.

1. hot + est = _____
2. clan + ish = _____
3. step + ing = _____
4. mad + ness = _____
5. sad + er = _____

6. water + ing = _____
7. stretch + er = _____
8. plan + ed = _____
9. form + ed = _____
10. snap + ed = _____

Part C

These words are in the puzzle. Circle 7 or more of the words.

serving sell arm
lone port vote
plan voice equal
game sign berry

```
s g i s i g n
s e r v i n g
b q l p o o a
e u v l o t m
r a o a a r e
r l o n e r t
y v o i c e m
```

Name _____ Date _____

Part D

Write the word for each meaning. The words will contain these morphographs:

ish	like	**en**	to make	**de**	away from, down
al	related to	**ful**	full of	**pre**	before

word   **meaning**

1. _____   full of hope

2. _____   to make wide

3. _____   press down

4. _____   like a child

5. _____   plan before

6. _____   related to rent

Part E

Figure out each word and write it in the blank below.

shwa   rreby   iiclv   adwnre

1. _____ 2. _____ 3. _____ 4. _____

Part F

Fill in the blanks to show the morphographs in each word.

1. _____ + _____ + _____ = playfully

2. _____ + _____ + _____ = designer

3. _____ + _____ = noting

4. _____ + _____ = notable

5. _____ + _____ + _____ = reserved

6. _____ + _____ + _____ = preplanned

PART	A	B	C	D	E	F	G	Worksheet Errors	Worksheet Points	Oral Points	Bonus Points	Total Points
										+	+	=

Lesson 36

Name _____ Date _____

Part A

1. _____   4. _____

2. _____   5. _____

3. _____   6. _____

Part B

1. _____ + _____ = _____

2. _____ + _____ = _____

3. _____ + _____ = _____

4. _____ + _____ = _____

Part C

Fill in the blanks to show the morphographs in each word.

1. _____ + _____ = shopping

2. _____ + _____ = widely

3. _____ + _____ = hopeless

4. _____ + _____ = cared

Part D

Make 6 real words from the morphographs in the box.

ed	er	rent	bare	ing	serve	dine

1. _____   4. _____

2. _____   5. _____

3. _____   6. _____

PART	A	B	C	D	E	F	G	Worksheet Errors	Worksheet Points	Oral Points	Bonus Points	Total Points
										+	+	=

Name _____ Date _____

Change the **y** to **i** when a word ends **consonant-and-y** and the next morphograph begins with anything except **i**.

Part A

1. _____   4. _____

2. _____   5. _____

3. _____

Part B

1. study + ed = _____   4. study + ing = _____

2. nasty + ness = _____   5. deal + er = _____

3. boy + ish = _____   6. happy + ness = _____

Part C

Make 15 real words from the morphographs in the box.

hope	use	ful	less	ly	care	rest

1. _____   9. _____

2. _____   10. _____

3. _____   11. _____

4. _____   12. _____

5. _____   13. _____

6. _____   14. _____

7. _____   15. _____

8. _____

Name _____ Date _____

Part D

Add these morphographs together. Some of the words follow the rule about doubling the final **c** in a short word.

1. big + est   = _____
2. mis + deal + ing = _____
3. sad + en   = _____
4. swim + er   = _____

5. run + ing   = _____
6. mad + ness   = _____
7. length + en   = _____
8. form + al + ly   = _____

Part E

Fill in the blanks to show the morphographs in each word.

1. _____ + _____ = biggest
2. _____ + _____ = planner
3. _____ + _____ = changing
4. _____ + _____ = dining
5. _____ + _____ = careful
6. _____ + _____ = barred
7. _____ + _____ = package
8. _____ + _____ = clannish

PART	A	B	C	D	E	F	G	Worksheet Errors	Worksheet Points	Oral Points	Bonus Points	Total Points
									+	+	=	

Lesson 38

Name _____ Date _____

Change the **y** to **i** when a word ends **consonant-and-y** and the next morphograph begins with anything except **i**.

Part A

1. _____   4. _____

2. _____   5. _____

3. _____

Part B

1. sturdy + ness   = _____   4. fancy + ful   = _____

2. dry + ing   = _____   5. play + ful   = _____

3. note + ed   = _____   6. hurry + ing   = _____

Part C

Make 8 real words from the morphographs in the box.

| de | er | fine | serve | light | ing | grade |

1. _____   5. _____

2. _____   6. _____

3. _____   7. _____

4. _____   8. _____

Part D

Add these morphographs together. Some of the words follow the rule about doubling the final **c** in a short word.

1. drop + ing   = _____   5. bar + ing   = _____

2. plan + ing   = _____   6. shop + less   = _____

3. length + en   = _____   7. hot + er   = _____

4. wash + er   = _____   8. step + ed   = _____

PART	A	B	C	D	E	F	G	Worksheet Errors	Worksheet Points	Oral Points	Bonus Points	Total Points
										+	+	=

Lesson 39

Name _____ Date _____

Change the **y** to **i** when a word ends **consonant-and-y** and the next morphograph begins with anything except **i**.

Part A

1. _____   5. _____

2. _____   6. _____

3. _____   7. _____

4. _____   8. _____

Part B

Add the morphographs together. Some of the words follow the rule about changing the **y** to **i** in a word.

1. boy + ish   = _____

2. sturdy + er   = _____

3. cry + er   = _____

4. dry + est   = _____

5. form + ing   = _____

6. copy + ed   = _____

Part C

Write **s** or **es** in the second column. Then add the morphographs together.

		s or es		new word
1. press	+	_____	=	_____
2. shop	+	_____	=	_____
3. buzz	+	_____	=	_____
4. stretch	+	_____	=	_____
5. form	+	_____	=	_____
6. deal	+	_____	=	_____

Name _____ Date _____

Part D

Make 11 real words from the morphographs in the box.
Some of the words follow the rule about doubling the final **c** in short words.

s	ed	snap	rest	shop	step	ing

1. _____   7. _____

2. _____   8. _____

3. _____   9. _____

4. _____   10. _____

5. _____   11. _____

6. _____

Part E

Fill in the blanks to show the morphographs in each word.

1. _____ + _____ = buzzer

2. _____ + _____ = civilly

3. _____ + _____ = dropper

4. _____ + _____ = strengthen

5. _____ + _____ = really

6. _____ + _____ + _____ = informer

PART	A	B	C	D	E	F	G	Worksheet Errors	Worksheet Points	Oral Points	Bonus Points	Total Points
									+	+	=	

Lesson 40

Name _____ Date _____

Change the **y** to **i** when a word ends **consonant-and-y** and the next morphograph begins with anything except **i**.

Part A

1. _____   4. _____

2. _____   5. _____

3. _____

Part B

Write **s** or **es** in the second column. Then add the morphographs together.

	s or **es**	**new word**
1. back +	_____ =	_____
2. match +	_____ =	_____
3. wash +	_____ =	_____
4. crash +	_____ =	_____

Part C

Add the morphographs together. Some of the words follow the rule about changing **y** to **i** in a word.

1. joy + ful   = _____   5. worry + ing   = _____

2. pity+ ful   = _____   6. worry + er   = _____

3. dry + er   = _____   7. cry + ing   = _____

4. human + ness = _____   8. play + er   = _____

Part D

1. _____

_____

2. _____

_____

Name _____ Date _____

Part E

Make 10 real words from the morphographs in the box.

er	ly	est	ness	mad	thick	sad

1. _____   6. _____

2. _____   7. _____

3. _____   8. _____

4. _____   9. _____

5. _____   10. _____

Part F

Write the word for each meaning. The words will contain these morphographs:

ish like   **con** with   **in** in; not   **de** down; away
al related to   **age** related to   **en** to make   **ful** full of

	word	**meaning**
1.	_____	related to form
2.	_____	sign with
3.	_____	take in
4.	_____	to make fresh
5.	_____	away from port
6.	_____	related to something packed
7.	_____	like a fool
8.	_____	full of use

PART	A	B	C	D	E	F	G	Worksheet Errors	Worksheet Points	Oral Points	Bonus Points	Total Points
										+	+	=

Lesson 41

Name _____ Date _____

Part A

1. _____   4. _____

2. _____   5. _____

3. _____   6. _____

Part B

Add the morphographs together. Some of the words follow the rule about changing the **y** to **i** in a word.

1. study + ed   = _____   5. water + ed   = _____

2. study + ing   = _____   6. sturdy + ness   = _____

3. fancy + ful   = _____   7. worry + er   = _____

4. cry + er   = _____   8. nasty + ness   = _____

Part C

Write **s** or **es** in the second column. Then add the morphographs together.

	s or **es**	**new word**
1. box	+ _____	= _____
2. buzz	+ _____	= _____
3. snap	+ _____	= _____
4. stretch	+ _____	= _____

Name _____ Date _____

Part D

Circle the misspelled word in each group. Then write it correctly in the blank.

1. world

   civel

   shining

   _____

2. happy

   motor

   auther

   _____

3. stretch

   choice

   forse

   _____

4. equil

   hopeful

   trace

   _____

5. depressing

   realy

   wrong

   _____

6. should

   could

   nasti

   _____

Part E

Make 8 real words from the morphographs in the box.

| stretch | stop | wash | snap | er | ed | ing |

1. _____   5. _____

2. _____   6. _____

3. _____   7. _____

4. _____   8. _____

Part F

Circle the words in the line.

1. (strength)   strenthstrengthstrethstrengthhstrengthstrestrength

2. (stretch)   stretchstrestretchstrechstretchchstretchsstretch

3. (friend)   frindfriendfrendfrienddfriendfreindfriendd friend

PART	A	B	C	D	E	F	G	Worksheet Errors	Worksheet Points	Oral Points	Bonus Points	Total Points
										+	+	=

Lesson 42

Name _____ Date _____

Part A

1. _____   4. _____

2. _____   5. _____

3. _____   6. _____

Part B

1. _____   5. _____

2. _____   6. _____

3. _____   7. _____

4. _____   8. _____

Part C

Make 5 real words from the morphographs in the box.

age	use	pack	ing	er

1. _____   4. _____

2. _____   5. _____

3. _____

Part D

Add the morphographs together. Some of the words follow the rule about changing the **y** to **i** in a word.

1. baby + ish   = _____   5. dry + ly   = _____

2. play + er   = _____   6. busy + ly   = _____

3. try + ing   = _____   7. buzz + er   = _____

4. hurry + ed   = _____   8. copy + er   = _____

Name _____ Date _____

Part E

Write **s** or **es** in the second column. Then add the morphographs together.

		s or **es**	**new word**
1. crash	+	_____	=	_____
2. fox	+	_____	=	_____
3. buzz	+	_____	=	_____
4. sign	+	_____	=	_____

Part F

Draw a line from the homonyms to their meanings.

homonym   **meaning**

right •   • correct; opposite of left

write •   • put words on paper

PART	A	B	C	D	E	F	G	Worksheet Errors	Worksheet Points	Oral Points	Bonus Points	Total Points
										+	+	=

Name _____ Date _____

Part A

1. _____   5. _____

2. _____   6. _____

3. _____   7. _____

4. _____

Part B

1. _____ + _____ = _____

2. _____ + _____ = _____

3. _____ + _____ = _____

4. _____ + _____ = _____

5. _____ + _____ = _____

6. _____ + _____ = _____

7. _____ + _____ = _____

8. _____ + _____ = _____

Part C

Make 7 real words from the morphographs in the box.

pack	age	bag	ed	ing

1. _____   5. _____

2. _____   6. _____

3. _____   7. _____

4. _____

Name _____ Date _____

Part D

Figure out each word and write it in the blank below.

thengstr   rreby   tiwre   throme

1. _____ 2. _____ 3. _____ 4. _____

Part E

Write **s** or **es** in the second column. Then add the morphographs together.

	s or **es**	**new word**

1. light   + _____ = _____

2. tax   + _____ = _____

3. buzz   + _____ = _____

4. press   + _____ = _____

5. run   + _____ = _____

6. box   + _____ = _____

Part F

Fill in the blanks to show the morphographs in each word.

1. _____ + _____ + _____ = conserving

2. _____ + _____ = biggest

3. _____ + _____ = wrapper

4. _____ + _____ = lately

5. _____ + _____ = shining

6. _____ + _____ + _____ = unchanging

PART	A	B	C	D	E	F	G	Worksheet Errors	Worksheet Points	Oral Points	Bonus Points	Total Points
										+	+	=

Lesson 44

Name _____ Date _____

Part A

Figure out the rule and write it. Remember to spell the words correctly.

and the next morphograph begins with **v** . . . when the word ends **cvc** . . . Double the final **c** in a short word

_____

_____

Part B

1. _____

_____

2. _____

_____

Part C

Circle the misspelled word in each group. Then write it correctly in the blank.

1. brother
   story
   shuld
   were

   _____

2. rong
   wrap
   nasty
   civil

   _____

3. shineing
   hurried
   joyful
   wander

   _____

4. stretch
   civilly
   realy
   unfilling

   _____

5. swimer
   runner
   berry
   restful

   _____

6. stretcher
   friendly
   unarmmed
   shopper

   _____

Name _____ Date _____

Part D

Add the morphographs together. Some of the words follow the rule about dropping the final **e.**

1. write + ing   = _____
2. safe + ly   = _____
3. late + er   = _____
4. lone + ly   = _____
5. force + ful   = _____
6. like + able   = _____
7. re + serve + ing = _____
8. note + able   = _____
9. change + ing   = _____
10. wide + ly   = _____

Part E

Circle each short word that ends **cvc.**
Remember: The letter **x** acts like two consonant letters.

stop	mad	rent	box
boy	plan	brother	play
hot	clan	water	fox
buzz	bar	bare	snap

PART	A	B	C	D	E	F	G	Worksheet Errors	Worksheet Points	Oral Points	Bonus Points	Total Points
										+	+	=

Lesson 45

Name _____ Date _____

Part A

Figure out the rules and write them. Remember to spell the words correctly.

1. a word when the next morphograph begins . . . Drop the final **e** from . . . with a vowel letter

   _____

   _____

2. **cvc** and the next . . . Double the final **c** . . . morphograph begins with **v** . . . in a short word when the word ends

   _____

   _____

Part B

Write each of these words in a box. Write "free space" in one box.

reserve   carry   equally   consign   forceful   safely   latest   should

informer   package   happiness   boyish   rise   lengthen   were

Part C

Add the morphographs together. Some of the words follow the rule about changing the y to i in a word.

1. study + ing   = _____
2. study + ed   = _____
3. dry + ly   = _____
4. dry + ed   = _____
5. dry + ing   = _____
6. baby + ish   = _____
7. dry + est   = _____
8. nasty + ness = _____
9. play + er   = _____
10. play + ing   = _____
11. play + ful   = _____
12. cry + er   = _____

Name _____ Date _____

Part D

Write **s** or **es** in the second column. Then add the morphographs together.

	s or **es**	**new word**

1. buzz   + _____ = _____

2. fan   + _____ = _____

3. brother   + _____ = _____

4. press   + _____ = _____

5. stretch   + _____ = _____

6. box   + _____ = _____

Part E

Fill in the blanks to show the morphographs in each word.

1. _____ + _____ + _____ + _____ = unrefreshed

2. _____ + _____ = dropping

3. _____ + _____ + _____ = hopelessness

4. _____ + _____ = passage

5. _____ + _____ + _____ = unfitting

6. _____ + _____ = shining

7. _____ + _____ + _____ = unnerving

8. _____ + _____ = equally

PART	A	B	C	D	E	F	G	Worksheet Errors	Worksheet Points	Oral Points	Bonus Points	Total Points
										+	+	=

Lesson 47

Name _____ Date _____

Part A

1. _____ + _____ = _____
2. _____ + _____ = _____
3. _____ + _____ = _____
4. _____ + _____ = _____
5. _____ + _____ = _____
6. _____ + _____ = _____

Part B

1. _____   4. _____
2. _____   5. _____
3. _____   6. _____

Part C

Make 10 real words from the morphographs in the box.
Some of the words will follow a rule, so be careful.

en	est	sad	mad	ness	wide	fine

1. _____   6. _____
2. _____   7. _____
3. _____   8. _____
4. _____   9. _____
5. _____   10. _____

Name _____ Date _____

Part (D)

Figure out the rules and write them. Remember to spell the words correctly.

1. word ends **cvc** and . . . Double the final **c** in . . . the next morphograph begins with **v** . . . a short word when the

   _____

   _____

2. word when the next . . . a vowel letter . . . morphograph begins with . . . Drop the final **e** from a

   _____

Part (E)

Fill in the blanks to show the morphographs in each word.

1. _____ + _____ = swimming

2. _____ + _____ + _____ = defacing

3. _____ + _____ = taken

4. _____ + _____ = sadden

5. _____ + _____ = choicest

6. _____ + _____ = forceful

7. _____ + _____ = racer

Bonus Exercise)

1. **carry**   carr __   car __ __   ca __ __ __   c __ __ __ __   __ __ __ __ __

2. **stretch**   str __ tch   st __ __ __ ch   s __ __ __ __ __ h   __ __ __ __ __ __ __ h

3. **change**   cha __ __ e   ch __ __ __ e   c __ __ __ __ __   __ __ __ __ __ __

PART	A	B	C	D	E	F	G	Worksheet Errors	Worksheet Points	Oral Points	Bonus Points	Total Points
										+	+	=

Lesson 48

Name _____ Date _____

Part A

1. _____   4. _____

2. _____   5. _____

3. _____   6. _____

Part B

Make 11 real words from the morphographs in the box.
Some of the words will follow a rule, so be careful.

er	use	grade	ing	stop	able	trap

1. _____   7. _____

2. _____   8. _____

3. _____   9. _____

4. _____   10. _____

5. _____   11. _____

6. _____

Part C

Add the morphographs together. Some of the words follow the rule about changing **y** to **i** in a word.

1. boy + ish   = _____   7. carry + er   = _____

2. sturdy + ness = _____   8. cry + ing   = _____

3. worry + ed   = _____   9. try + al   = _____

4. pity + ful   = _____   10. deny + al   = _____

5. baby + ish   = _____   11. stay + ed   = _____

6. farm + ing   = _____   12. fly + er   = _____

Name _____ Date _____

Part D

These words are in the puzzle.
Circle 7 or more of the words.

civil	verb	carry
might	deny	robber
gone	dine	match
mad	does	easy

```
c i v i l r
m a d e r o
a i r i r b
t d g r n b
c e o h y e
h n n e t r
m y e a s y
```

Part E

Fill in the blanks to show the morphographs in each word.

1. _____ + _____ = buzzes

2. _____ + _____ = barring

3. _____ + _____ = lonely

4. _____ + _____ = writing

5. _____ + _____ = signal

6. _____ + _____ = snapped

7. _____ + _____ + _____ = reserving

PART	A	B	C	D	E	F	G	Worksheet Errors	Worksheet Points	Oral Points	Bonus Points	Total Points
										+	+	=

Lesson 49

Name _____ Date _____

Part A

1. _____   4. _____

2. _____   5. _____

3. _____

Part B

1. could not   = _____   5. he will   = _____

2. should not   = _____   6. would not = _____

3. she is   = _____   7. I have   = _____

4. is not   = _____   8. you will   = _____

Part C

1. _____

_____

2. _____

_____

Part D

1. _____ + _____ = _____

2. _____ + _____ = _____

3. _____ + _____ = _____

4. _____ + _____ = _____

5. _____ + _____ = _____

6. _____ + _____ = _____

7. _____ + _____ = _____

8. _____ + _____ = _____

Name _____ Date _____

Part E

Make 11 real words from the morphographs in the box.

| ing | shop | ful | hate | run | ed | er | hope |

1. _____   7. _____

2. _____   8. _____

3. _____   9. _____

4. _____   10. _____

5. _____   11. _____

6. _____

Part F

Circle the misspelled word in each group.
Then write it correctly in the blank.

1. other
   cary
   wrong
   could

   _____

2. story
   mispell
   sturdy
   fancy

   _____

3. whether
   strength
   serve
   strech

   _____

4. author
   mother
   buz
   civil

   _____

PART	A	B	C	D	E	F	G	Worksheet Errors	Worksheet Points	Oral Points	Bonus Points	Total Points
										+	+	=

Lesson 50

Name _____ Date _____

Part A

1. _____   4. _____

2. _____   5. _____

3. _____   6. _____

Part B

Write contractions for the words in the first column.

	contraction		contraction
1. were not	= _____	5. you have	= _____
2. does not	= _____	6. did not	= _____
3. are not	= _____	7. can not	= _____
4. she will	= _____	8. they are	= _____

Part C

Make 10 real words from the morphographs in the box.
Some of the words follow the rule about changing **y** to **i** in a word.

ful	ing	play	fancy	ed	er	pity

1. _____   6. _____

2. _____   7. _____

3. _____   8. _____

4. _____   9. _____

5. _____   10. _____

PART	A	B	C	D	E	F	G	Worksheet Errors	Worksheet Points	Oral Points	Bonus Points	Total Points
										+	+	=

Lesson **51**

Name _____ Date _____

Part A

1. _____   4. _____

2. _____   5. _____

3. _____

Part B

1. _____

_____

2. _____

_____

Part C

Make 11 real words from the morphographs in the box.

est	nasty	er	ly	busy	dry	sturdy

1. _____   7. _____

2. _____   8. _____

3. _____   9. _____

4. _____   10. _____

5. _____   11. _____

6. _____

Part D

Add these morphographs together.

1. swim + er   = _____

2. fine + est   = _____

3. wide + est   = _____

4. con + sign   = _____

5. mad + ly   = _____

6. rage + ing   = _____

7. trap + er   = _____

8. un + civil + ly   = _____

Name _____ Date _____

Part E

Write the word for each meaning. The words will contain these morphographs.

al   related to   **ful**   full of   **est**   the most

pre   before   **ish**   like   **en**   to make

	word	meaning
1.	_____	like a baby
2.	_____	the most late
3.	_____	related to signs
4.	_____	wrap before
5.	_____	make light
6.	_____	full of care

Part F

Write contractions for the words in the first column.

		contraction			contraction
1. let us	=	_____	5. we have	=	_____
2. have not	=	_____	6. what is	=	_____
3. was not	=	_____	7. he is	=	_____
4. they will	=	_____	8. would not	=	_____

PART	A	B	C	D	E	F	G	Worksheet Errors	Worksheet Points	Oral Points	Bonus Points	Total Points
										+	+	=

Name _____ Date _____

Part A

Complete each sentence correctly with one of these words:

write   right

1. My grandmother likes it when I _____ long letters.

2. Janis is the _____ person for the job.

3. My answers on the test were all _____ .

4. When Martin was four years old, he could _____ his name.

Part B

Write contractions for the words in the first column.

	contraction			contraction
1. has not	= _____	5. I will	=	_____
2. you are	= _____	6. they are	=	_____
3. we will	= _____	7. were not	=	_____
4. are not	= _____	8. it is	=	_____

Part C

Make 10 real words from the morphographs in the box.

deny	stay	ing	ed	able	dry	vary

1. _____   6. _____

2. _____   7. _____

3. _____   8. _____

4. _____   9. _____

5. _____   10. _____

Name _____ Date _____

Part D

Circle the misspelled word in each group.
Then write it correctly in the blank.

1. worry

   might

   brother

   civel

   _____

2. catch

   friend

   wandor

   change

   _____

3. hurring

   fitness

   whether

   woman

   _____

4. claim

   queit

   choice

   equal

   _____

Part E

Fill in the blanks to show the morphographs in each word.

1. _____ + _____ + _____ + _____ = unrefined

2. _____ + _____ + _____ = packaging

3. _____ + _____ + _____ = rightfully

4. _____ + _____ = inhuman

5. _____ + _____ + _____ = strengthening

6. _____ + _____ = lonely

7. _____ + _____ + _____ = helpfulness

8. _____ + _____ + _____ = unequally

9. _____ + _____ + _____ = resigned

10. _____ + _____ + _____ + _____ = unrelated

PART	A	B	C	D	E	F	G	Worksheet Errors	Worksheet Points	Oral Points	Bonus Points	Total Points
										+	+	=

Lesson 53

Name _____ Date _____

Part A

1. _____   4. _____
2. _____   5. _____
3. _____   6. _____

Part B

1. _____   7. _____
2. _____   8. _____
3. _____   9. _____
4. _____   10. _____
5. _____   11. _____
6. _____   12. _____

Part C

Write contractions for the words in the first column.

	contraction		contraction
1. should not	= _____	4. what is	= _____
2. she is	= _____	5. they will	= _____
3. I have	= _____	6. we are	= _____

Part D

Make 8 real words from the morphographs in the box.

sound	ness	ly	est	happy	nasty

1. _____   5. _____
2. _____   6. _____
3. _____   7. _____
4. _____   8. _____

Name _____ Date _____

Part E

Figure out the rules and write them. Remember to spell the words correctly.

1. in a short word when the . . . next morphograph begins with **v** . . . Double the final **c** . . . word ends **cvc** and the

    _____

    _____

2. a **consonant-and-y** and the . . . a word when the word ends with . . . next morphograph begins with anything except **i** . . . Change the **y** to **i** in

    _____

    _____

PART	A	B	C	D	E	F	G	Worksheet Errors	Worksheet Points	Oral Points	Bonus Points	Total Points
										+	+	=

Lesson **54**

Part **A**

1. _____ + _____ = _____
2. _____ + _____ = _____
3. _____ + _____ = _____
4. _____ + _____ = _____
5. _____ + _____ = _____
6. _____ + _____ = _____
7. _____ + _____ = _____
8. _____ + _____ = _____

Part **B**

1. _____   5. _____
2. _____   6. _____
3. _____   7. _____
4. _____   8. _____

Part **C**

1. _____

_____

2. _____

_____

Name _____ Date _____

Part D

Make 10 real words from the morphographs in the box.

| friend | ly | happy | ness | lone | sturdy | est |

1. _____   6. _____

2. _____   7. _____

3. _____   8. _____

4. _____   9. _____

5. _____   10. _____

Part E

Write the contractions for the words in the first column.

contraction   **contraction**

1. can not   = _____   5. are not   = _____

2. does not   = _____   6. what is   = _____

3. they will   = _____   7. it is   = _____

4. you have   = _____   8. let us   = _____

Part F

Fill in the blanks to show the morphographs in each word.

1. _____ + _____ = sadder

2. _____ + _____ = strengthen

3. _____ + _____ = useful

PART	A	B	C	D	E	F	G	Worksheet Errors	Worksheet Points	Oral Points	Bonus Points	Total Points
										+	+	=

Name _____ Date _____

Part A

1. _____ + _____ = _____
2. _____ + _____ = _____
3. _____ + _____ = _____
4. _____ + _____ = _____
5. _____ + _____ = _____
6. _____ + _____ = _____
7. _____ + _____ = _____
8. _____ + _____ = _____

Part B

Part C

Add these morphographs together. Some of the words follow the rule about dropping the final **e.** Some of the words follow the rule about doubling.

1. re + move + al   = _____
2. in + come   = _____
3. rise + ing   = _____
4. safe + ly   = _____
5. hot + est   = _____
6. mad + ness   = _____

7. un + de + serve + ing = _____
8. use + age   = _____
9. verb + al + ly   = _____
10. re + cent + ly   = _____
11. swim + er   = _____
12. real + ly   = _____

Name _____ Date _____

Part D

These words are in the puzzle.
Circle 7 or more of the words.

brotherly	report	spotted
race	neat	traps
stay	loud	vary
whether	length	cared

```
b  r  c  l  s  n  t  l  w
r  r  u  a  o  u  u  e  h
s  e  o  n  r  u  o  n  e
s  p  o  t  t  e  d  g  t
s  o  a  y  h  n  d  t  h
s  r  a  c  e  e  e  h  e
l  t  r  a  p  s  r  a  r
v  t  a  t  o  r  t  l  t
v  a  r  y  y  r  h  h  y
```

Part E

Complete each sentence correctly with one of these words:

vary   write   right   whole

1. Tony's new shoes are exactly the _____ size.

2. Instead of eating the same thing all the time, you should _____ your diet.

3. My uncle was so hungry last Sunday that he ate a _____ chicken.

4. Joggers don't usually run at the same speed all the time. They usually

   _____ their pace.

5. The blanks on your worksheet are where you _____ spelling words.

6. Last Friday we worked hard the _____ day.

PART	A	B	C	D	E	F	G	Worksheet Errors	Worksheet Points	Oral Points	Bonus Points	Total Points
										+	+	=

Name _____ Date _____

Part A

		s or es	new word			s or es	new word

1. worry   + _____ = _____   6. boy   + _____ = _____

2. story   + _____ = _____   7. play   + _____ = _____

3. try   + _____ = _____   8. study + _____ = _____

4. joy   + _____ = _____   9. stay   + _____ = _____

5. copy   + _____ = _____   10. carry + _____ = _____

Part B

1. _____   4. _____

2. _____   5. _____

3. _____

Part C

1. _____   5. _____

2. _____   6. _____

3. _____   7. _____

4. _____

Name _____ Date _____

Part D

Circle the misspelled word in each group. Then write it correctly in the blank.

1. proud

   mispell

   wrong

   _____

2. wander

   equil

   civil

   _____

3. auther

   hurry

   whether

   _____

4. pleaze

   straight

   whose

   _____

5. file

   happiness

   realy

   _____

6. sirve

   farmer

   fancy

   _____

Part E

Fill in the blanks to show the morphographs in each word.

1. _____ + _____ = conform

2. _____ + _____ = consign

3. _____ + _____ = reserve

4. _____ + _____ + _____ = conserving

5. _____ + _____ = inform

Bonus Exercise

1. **straight** str _ _ ght   str _ _ _ _ t   s _ _ _ _ _ _ t

   _ _ _ _ _ _ _

2. **strength** str _ _ gth   s _ _ _ _ _ _ h   _ _ _ _ _ _ _

PART	A	B	C	D	E	F	G	Worksheet Errors	Worksheet Points	Oral Points	Bonus Points	Total Points
										+	+	=

Lesson 58

Name _____ Date _____

Part A

		s or es	new word				s or es	new word
1.	stay	+ _____	= _____		5.	worry	+ _____	= _____
2.	copy	+ _____	= _____		6.	fly	+ _____	= _____
3.	toy	+ _____	= _____		7.	boy	+ _____	= _____
4.	spray	+ _____	= _____		8.	carry	+ _____	= _____

Part B

1. _____   3. _____

2. _____   4. _____

Part C

Fill in the blanks to show the morphographs in each word.

1. _____ + _____ = proclaim

2. _____ + _____ = express

3. _____ + _____ = profuse

4. _____ + _____ = profit

5. _____ + _____ = consign

6. _____ + _____ = conserve

7. _____ + _____ = relate

Name _____ Date _____

Part D

Figure out the rules and write them. Remember to spell the words correctly.

1. next morphograph begins with … Drop the **final e** … a vowel letter … from a word when the

_____

_____

2. next morphograph begins with **v** … short word when the … Double the final **c** in a …
   word ends **cvc** and the

_____

_____

Part E

Add these morphographs together. Some of the words follow spelling rules.

1. vary + ed   = _____
2. rise + ing   = _____
3. trap + er   = _____
4. study + ing   = _____
5. straight + en   = _____
6. strength + en   = _____
7. nasty + ly   = _____
8. lone + ly   = _____
9. un + equal + ly = _____
10. human + ness   = _____
11. dine + ing   = _____
12. force + ful   = _____

PART	A	B	C	D	E	F	G	Worksheet Errors	Worksheet Points	Oral Points	Bonus Points	Total Points
										+	+	=

Name _____ Date _____

Part A

		s or es		new word			s or es		new word
1. boy	+	_____	=	_____	5. baby	+	_____	=	_____
2. story	+	_____	=	_____	6. fly	+	_____	=	_____
3. try	+	_____	=	_____	7. berry	+	_____	=	_____
4. worry	+	_____	=	_____	8. carry	+	_____	=	_____

Part B

1. _____   3. _____

2. _____   4. _____

Part C

1. _____   4. _____

2. _____   5. _____

3. _____

Part D

Write contractions for the words in the first column.

		contraction			contraction
1. were not	=	_____	5. let us	=	_____
2. have not	=	_____	6. are not	=	_____
3. you will	=	_____	7. would not	=	_____
4. they had	=	_____	8. does not	=	_____

Name _____ Date _____

Part E

Complete each sentence correctly with one of these words:

write   vary   whole   very   right   hole

1. Parachute jumping is a _____ exciting sport.

2. Whenever you misspell a word, you should _____ that word correctly at least one time.

3. A woodpecker made a small _____ in the side of our barn.

4. I like to do a different set of exercises every day. My friends also _____ their exercises.

5. No one thought Sandy would finish her book, but she read the _____ story anyway.

6. The Marche Company hasn't hired a shipping clerk because they haven't found the

    _____ person for the job.

Part F

Fill in the blanks to show the morphographs in each word.

1. _____ + _____ = relate

2. _____ + _____ + _____ = actively

3. _____ + _____ + _____ = expressive

4. _____ + _____ + _____ = relative

5. _____ + _____ + _____ = inactive

6. _____ + _____ + _____ = removal

7. _____ + _____ + _____ = remaining

8. _____ + _____ = signal

PART	A	B	C	D	E	F	G	Worksheet Errors	Worksheet Points	Oral Points	Bonus Points	Total Points
										+	+	=

Lesson 60

Name _____ Date _____

Part A

	s or **es**	new word		**s** or **es**	new word
1. study	+ _____	= _____	4. cry	+ _____	= _____
2. story	+ _____	= _____	5. joy	+ _____	= _____
3. play	+ _____	= _____	6. city	+ _____	= _____

Part B

1. _____   5. _____

2. _____   6. _____

3. _____   7. _____

4. _____   8. _____

Part C

1. _____   3. _____

2. _____   4. _____

Part D

Make 8 real words from the morphographs in the box.
Some of the words follow the doubling rule. Some of the words follow the **y-to-i** rule.

hot	ly	sturdy	er	mad	est

1. _____   5. _____

2. _____   6. _____

3. _____   7. _____

4. _____   8. _____

PART	A	B	C	D	E	F	G	Worksheet Errors	Worksheet Points	Oral Points	Bonus Points	Total Points
										+	+	=

Lesson 61

Name _____ Date _____

Part A

1. _____   4. _____

2. _____   5. _____

3. _____

Part B

	s or es	new word			s or es	new word
1. copy	+ _____	= _____	5. city	+ _____	= _____
2. spray	+ _____	= _____	6. worry	+ _____	= _____
3. fly	+ _____	= _____	7. study	+ _____	= _____
4. boy	+ _____	= _____	8. story	+ _____	= _____

Part C

1. _____

2. _____

3. _____

4. _____

Part D

Draw a line from each word to its meaning.

very •   • all parts together

right •   • put words on paper

vary •   • an empty space

whole •   • really

write •   • correct; opposite of left

hole •   • change

PART	A	B	C	D	E	F	G	Worksheet Errors	Worksheet Points	Oral Points	Bonus Points	Total Points
										+	+	=

Lesson 62

Name _____ Date _____

Part A

1. _____   6. _____
2. _____   7. _____
3. _____   8. _____
4. _____   9. _____
5. _____   10. _____

Part B

1. _____

_____

2. _____

_____

Part C

Write the contractions for the words in the first column.

	contraction		contraction
1. what is	= _____	4. he will	= _____
2. would not	= _____	5. are not	= _____
3. can not	= _____	6. it is	= _____

Part D

Write **s** or **es** in the second column. Then add the morphographs together.

	s or es	new word		s or es	new word
1. tax	+ _____	= _____	5. copy	+ _____	= _____
2. study	+ _____	= _____	6. thought	+ _____	= _____
3. play	+ _____	= _____	7. worry	+ _____	= _____
4. brush	+ _____	= _____	8. spray	+ _____	= _____

98   Lesson 62

Name _____ Date _____

Part

Figure out the rules and write them. Remember to spell the words correctly.

1. **c** in a short word when . . . morphograph begins with **v** . . . the word ends . . . double the final . . . **cvc** and the next

   _____

   _____

2. a word when the word ends with . . . next morphograph begins with anything except **i** . . . a **consonant-and-y** and the . . . change the **y** to **i** in

   _____

   _____

Part F

Draw a line from each word to its meaning.

write   •   • all parts together

hole   •   • really

whole   •   • put words on paper

vary   •   • correct; opposite of left

right   •   • change

very   •   • an empty space

PART	A	B	C	D	E	F	G	Worksheet Errors	Worksheet Points	Oral Points	Bonus Points	Total Points
									+	+	=	

Lesson 63

Name _____ Date _____

Part A

1. _____   5. _____

2. _____   6. _____

3. _____   7. _____

4. _____   8. _____

Part B

Fill in the blanks to show the morphographs in each word.

1. _____ + _____ + _____ = repression

2. _____ + _____ + _____ + _____ = uninformed

3. _____ + _____ + _____ = inactive

4. _____ + _____ + _____ = thoughtlessly

5. _____ + _____ = foxes

6. _____ + _____ = berries

7. _____ + _____ + _____ = joyfully

8. _____ + _____ + _____ = replacing

Part C

Look at the last three letters of each word.
Make a **v** or a **c** above each of the last three letters.
Circle each short word that ends **cvc.**

1. under   3. grow   5. fur   7. show   9. whether

2. boy   4. fit   6. snap   8. bar   10. stay

Name _____ Date _____

Part D

Add these morphographs together. Remember to use your spelling rules.

1. please + ing = _____
2. worry + es = _____
3. neat + ness = _____
4. study + ing = _____
5. sad + ness = _____

6. re + late + ive = _____
7. story + es = _____
8. fit + ing = _____
9. pity + ful = _____
10. wrap + er = _____

Part E

Draw a line from each word to its meaning.

vary •   • all parts together

whole •   • something hard to do

right •   • change

write •   • correct; opposite of left

very •   • really

feat •   • an empty space

hole •   • put words on paper

PART	A	B	C	D	E	F	G	Worksheet Errors	Worksheet Points	Oral Points	Bonus Points	Total Points
										+	+	=

Lesson 64

Name _____ Date _____

Part A

1. _____   6. _____
2. _____   7. _____
3. _____   8. _____
4. _____   9. _____
5. _____   10. _____

Part B

1. _____ + _____ = _____
2. _____ + _____ = _____
3. _____ + _____ = _____
4. _____ + _____ = _____
5. _____ + _____ = _____
6. _____ + _____ = _____
7. _____ + _____ = _____
8. _____ + _____ = _____
9. _____ + _____ = _____
10. _____ + _____ = _____

Part C

Complete each sentence correctly with one of these words:

feat   write   whole   vary

1. The detective wasn't able to solve his case until he heard the _____ story.

2. Jan swam across the raging river, which was a brave _____ .

3. I used to always print my name, but now I _____ it.

4. The restaurants on Miller Street are popular because they _____ their menus daily.

5. A strongman at the circus performed a different _____ of strength during every intermission.

Name _____ Date _____

Part D

Make 11 real words from the morphographs in the box.

less	thought	ness	hope	ly	ful

1. _____
2. _____
3. _____
4. _____
5. _____
6. _____

7. _____
8. _____
9. _____
10. _____
11. _____

Part E

Add these morphographs together. Remember to use your spelling rules.

1. un + happy + ly   = _____
2. care + less + ly   = _____
3. snap + er   = _____
4. deny + al   = _____
5. lone + ly   = _____
6. ex + claim + ed   = _____
7. stop + age   = _____
8. re + move + al   = _____

PART	A	B	C	D	E	F	G	Worksheet Errors	Worksheet Points	Oral Points	Bonus Points	Total Points
										+	+	=

Lesson 65

Name _____ Date _____

Part A

1. _____ + _____ = _____
2. _____ + _____ = _____
3. _____ + _____ = _____
4. _____ + _____ = _____

Part B

1. _____ 3. _____
2. _____ 4. _____

Part C

1. _____ 4. _____
2. _____ 5. _____
3. _____ 6. _____

Part D

Fill in the blanks to show the morphographs in each word.

1. _____ + _____ = passion
2. _____ + _____ = passive
3. _____ + _____ = action
4. _____ + _____ = active
5. _____ + _____ = proverb
6. _____ + _____ = export
7. _____ + _____ = profound
8. _____ + _____ = exact

Name _____ Date _____

Part E

Circle the misspelled word in each group.
Then write it correctly in the blank.

1. fluid
   poison
   strate
   about
   _____

2. glory
   pleaze
   place
   civil
   _____

3. brother
   wrong
   carry
   hopeing
   _____

4. proud
   whose
   berry
   wurry
   _____

5. queit
   stretch
   friend
   wander
   _____

6. choice
   equil
   strength
   studying
   _____

7. studyes
   author
   neatly
   depressed
   _____

8. swimmer
   serving
   pitiful
   maddness
   _____

PART	A	B	C	D	E	F	G	Worksheet Errors	Worksheet Points	Oral Points	Bonus Points	Total Points
										+	+	=

Lesson 66

Name _____ Date _____

Part A

1. _____   3. _____

2. _____   4. _____

Part B

1. _____   3. _____

2. _____   4. _____

Part C

Write **s** or **es** in the second column. Then add the morphographs together.

	s or **es**	**new word**			**s** or **es**	**new word**
1. glory	+ _____	= _____	4. buzz	+ _____	= _____
2. stay	+ _____	= _____	5. joy	+ _____	= _____
3. press	+ _____	= _____	6. deny	+ _____	= _____

Part D

Fill in the blanks to show the morphographs in each word.

1. _____ + _____ = repress

2. _____ + _____ + _____ = repression

3. _____ + _____ + _____ = repressive

4. _____ + _____ + _____ = expression

Part E

Add these morphographs together. Remember to use your spelling rules.

1. strength + en + ing = _____   3. trap + er   = _____

2. poison + ed   = _____   4. happy + ness   = _____

PART	A	B	C	D	E	F	G	Worksheet Errors	Worksheet Points	Oral Points	Bonus Points	Total Points
										+	+	=

Lesson 67

Name _____ Date _____

Part A

1. _____ + _____ = _____
2. _____ + _____ = _____
3. _____ + _____ = _____
4. _____ + _____ = _____

Part B

1. _____ 4. _____

2. _____ 5. _____

3. _____ 6 _____

Part C

1. _____ 5. _____

2. _____ 6 _____

3. _____ 7. _____

4. _____ 8. _____

Part D

Draw a line from each word to its meaning.

write •   • really

vary •   • body parts

feat •   • correct; opposite of left

whole •   • put words on paper

very •   • all parts together

right •   • an empty space

feet •   • change

hole •   • something hard to do

Name _____ Date _____

Part E

Fill in the blanks to show the morphographs in each word.

1. _____ + _____ = preside

2. _____ + _____ = action

3. _____ + _____ = pressure

4. _____ + _____ = passive

5. _____ + _____ + _____ = relative

6. _____ + _____ = active

7. _____ + _____ = poisonous

8. _____ + _____ = feature

9. _____ + _____ + _____ = gloriously

10. _____ + _____ + _____ = formally

PART	A	B	C	D	E	F	G	Worksheet Errors	Worksheet Points	Oral Points	Bonus Points	Total Points
										+	+	=

Name _____ Date _____

Part A

1. _____   6. _____
2. _____   7. _____
3. _____   8. _____
4. _____   9. _____
5. _____   10. _____

Part B

Write each of these words in a box. Write "free space" in one box.

equally	defile	motherly	ruinous
studies	blow	depression	texture
preserve	feature	straight	various
they're	passion	babies	

(word bank: equally, defile, motherly, ruinous, studies, blow, depression, texture, preserve, feature, straight, various, they're, passion, babies)

Part C

Write s or es in the second column. Then add the morphographs together.

	s or es	new word		s or es	new word
1. cry	+ _____	= _____	5. story	+ _____	= _____
2. box	+ _____	= _____	6. friend	+ _____	= _____
3. vary	+ _____	= _____	7. glory	+ _____	= _____
4. stay	+ _____	= _____	8. play	+ _____	= _____

Name _____ Date _____

Part D

Circle the misspelled word in each group. Then write it correctly in the blank.

1. strength

   poisen

   fluid

   thought

   _____

2. worryes

   wrong

   studies

   brother

   _____

3. straight

   count

   realy

   change

   _____

4. friendly

   quietly

   author

   sturdyly

   _____

5. woman

   fansy

   copies

   swimmer

   _____

6. preserving

   joyously

   equall

   civilly

   _____

PART	A	B	C	D	E	F	G	Worksheet Errors	Worksheet Points	Oral Points	Bonus Points	Total Points
										+	+	=

Lesson 69

Name _____ Date _____

Part A

1. _____ 4. _____

2. _____ 5. _____

3. _____

Part B

1. _____

_____

2. _____

_____

Part C

1. _____ 5. _____

2. _____ 6. _____

3. _____ 7. _____

4. _____ 8. _____

Part D

Make 11 real words from the morphographs in the box.

est	happy	wide	ly	fine	ness	mad

1. _____ 7. _____

2. _____ 8. _____

3. _____ 9. _____

4. _____ 10. _____

5. _____ 11. _____

6. _____

Name _____ Date _____

Part E

Fill in the blanks to show the morphographs in each word.

1. _____ + _____ + _____ = protective
2. _____ + _____ + _____ = injection
3. _____ + _____ + _____ = progressed
4. _____ + _____ + _____ = reception
5. _____ + _____ = texture
6. _____ + _____ = feature
7. _____ + _____ = passion
8. _____ + _____ = studying
9. _____ + _____ = studious
10. _____ + _____ = signal

Part F

Circle the words in the lines.

1. (prove)   provprovepruveproreproveprproveeprov
2. (thought)   thoughtthouhgtthoughttthoughtthoughttthought
3. (straight)   straihgtstraightsstraightstraightstraigth
4. (whether)   whetherwetherwhetherwhwhetherwhethrwhether

PART	A	B	C	D	E	F	G	Worksheet Errors	Worksheet Points	Oral Points	Bonus Points	Total Points
										+	+	=

Lesson 70

Name _____ Date _____

Part A

1. _____   4. _____

2. _____   5. _____

3. _____

Part B

1. _____   5. _____

2. _____   6. _____

3. _____   7. _____

4. _____   8. _____

Part C

Add these morphographs together. Remember to use your spelling rules.

1. poison + ous   = _____

2. re + gain + ed   = _____

3. pause + ing   = _____

4. un + prove + en   = _____

5. fur + y   = _____

6. re + fuse + al   = _____

7. in + act + ion   = _____

8. ex + press + ive   = _____

9. fuse + ion   = _____

10. mis + place + ed   = _____

11. pro + claim + ed   = _____

12. spray + ed   = _____

13. please + ure   = _____

14. friend + ly + ness   = _____

15. carry + ed   = _____

Name _____ Date _____

Part D

Circle the misspelled word in each group.
Then write it correctly in the blank.

1. giving	2. fluids	3. brain	4. feature
detect	varies	reseptive	loudness
lenght	concept	pressure	dineing
hurried	furyous	washes	except

_____ _____ _____ _____

Part E

Fill in the blanks to show the morphographs in each word.

1. _____ + _____ = extent

2. _____ + _____ = content

3. _____ + _____ + _____ = intention

4. _____ + _____ = reside

5. _____ + _____ = inside

6. _____ + _____ = proven

PART	A	B	C	D	E	F	G	Worksheet Errors	Worksheet Points	Oral Points	Bonus Points	Total Points
										+	+	=

Lesson 71

Name _____ Date _____

Part A

1. _____   4. _____
2. _____   5. _____
3. _____   6. _____

Part B

1. _____   5. _____
2. _____   6. _____
3. _____   7. _____
4. _____   8. _____

Part C

1. _____ = reporting
2. _____ = photograph
3. _____ = intent
4. _____ = content
5. _____ = cloudy
6. _____ = poisonous
7. _____ = strengthening
8. _____ = physics

Name _____ Date _____

Part D

These words are in the puzzle.
Circle 7 or more of the words.

poison	found	photo
pound	concept	flat
lone	pity	whose
store	fact	proven

```
p  p  w  h  o  s  e  f
p  o  i  s  o  n  s  p
c  o  n  c  e  p  t  r
f  o  u  n  d  h  o  o
a  l  o  n  e  o  r  v
c  p  a  r  d  t  e  e
t  p  i  t  y  o  e  n
```

Part E

Add these morphographs together. Remember to use your spelling rules.

1. fury + ous = _____
2. pain + less + ly = _____
3. pro + gress + ive = _____
4. sore + ness = _____
5. text + ure + ed = _____
6. story + es = _____
7. please + ure = _____
8. hot + est = _____
9. force + ful = _____
10. ex + act + ly = _____
11. pro + found + ly = _____
12. feat + ure = _____

PART	A	B	C	D	E	F	G	Worksheet Errors	Worksheet Points	Oral Points	Bonus Points	Total Points
										+	+	=

Name _____ Date _____

Part Ⓐ

1. _____   4. _____

2. _____   5. _____

3. _____   6. _____

Part Ⓑ

1. _____   5. _____

2. _____   6. _____

3. _____   7. _____

4. _____   8. _____

Part Ⓒ

1. _____   5. _____

2. _____   6. _____

3. _____   7. _____

4. _____   8. _____

Part Ⓓ

Complete each sentence correctly with one of these words:

hole   right   varied   features   write

1. Murphy's Cafe _____ fried chicken every Friday.

2. Caron's experiment failed, but she had the _____ idea.

3. The markings on Holly's puppies _____ greatly.

4. Our boat won't float because it has a large _____ in the bottom.

5. Because our new car doesn't run well, we are going to _____ a letter to the company that made it.

Name _____ Date _____

Part **E**

Fill in the blanks to show the morphographs in each word.
Write the morphographs with plus signs in between them.

1. _____ = physical

2. _____ = physics

3. _____ = famous

4. _____ = photography

5. _____ = consent

6. _____ = regain

7. _____ = resent

8. _____ = spinner

9. _____ = retained

10. _____ = concept

PART	A	B	C	D	E	F	G	Worksheet Errors	Worksheet Points	Oral Points	Bonus Points	Total Points
										+	+	=

Lesson 74

Name _____ Date _____

Part A

Part B

1. _____ + _____ = _____
2. _____ + _____ = _____
3. _____ + _____ = _____
4. _____ + _____ = _____

Part C

Circle each short word that ends **cvc.**

Remember: **y** and **w** are vowels at the end of a morphograph.

          x acts like two consonant letters.

          short words have 3 or 4 letters.

1. gain	4. woman	7. boy	10. trap
2. know	5. man	8. box	11. brother
3. spin	6. show	9. swim	12. win

Name _____   Date _____

Part D

Add these morphographs together. Remember your spelling rules.

1. happy + ness   = _____

2. ease + y   = _____

3. thought + ful   = _____

4. spin + ing   = _____

5. sure + ly   = _____

6. dis + prove + en = _____

7. feat + ure   = _____

8. trap + er   = _____

Part E

Fill in the blanks to show the morphographs in each word.
Write the morphographs with plus signs in between them.

1. _____ = resign

2. _____ = signal

3. _____ = relate

4. _____ = busily

5. _____ = receptive

6. _____ = relative

7. _____ = pleasing

8. _____ = pleasure

PART	A	B	C	D	E	F	G	Worksheet Errors	Worksheet Points	Oral Points	Bonus Points	Total Points
										+	+	=

Lesson 75

Name _____ Date _____

Part A

1. _____   7. _____
2. _____   8. _____
3. _____   9. _____
4. _____   10. _____
5. _____   11. _____
6. _____   12. _____

Part B

1. _____   3. _____
2. _____   4. _____

Part C

Make 9 real words from the morphographs in the box.

ly	glory	nerve	ous	joy	study	vary

1. _____   6. _____
2. _____   7. _____
3. _____   8. _____
4. _____   9. _____
5. _____

Name _____ Date _____

Part D

Draw a line from each word to its meaning.

cent •   • something hard to do

feat •   • correct; opposite of left

vary •   • put words on paper

whole •   • one hundred

write •   • change

very •   • really

right •   • all parts together

Part E

**Circle the misspelled word in each group.
Then write it correctly in the blank.**

1. proove   2. civil   3. fone   4. could'nt

   phone   thoughtful   brain   trapper

   shore   starrless   shouldn't   studies

   straight   graph   wrong   lately

   _____   _____   _____   _____

PART	A	B	C	D	E	F	G	Worksheet Errors	Worksheet Points	Oral Points	Bonus Points	Total Points
										+	+	=

Lesson 76

Name _____ Date _____

Part A

1. _____   3. _____

2. _____   4. _____

Part B

1. _____

_____

2. _____

_____

Part C

The woman put the boxs of poisen in a
safe plase.   _____

_____

We spraied the moter with cleaning fluid. _____

_____

_____

Part D

Write s or es in the second column. Then add the morphographs together.

	s or es	new word		s or es	new word
1. spray	+ _____ = _____		5. stretch	+ _____ = _____	
2. catch	+ _____ = _____		6. hurry	+ _____ = _____	
3. vary	+ _____ = _____		7. stay	+ _____ = _____	
4. dry	+ _____ = _____		8. fry	+ _____ = _____	

PART	A	B	C	D	E	F	G	Worksheet Errors	Worksheet Points	Oral Points	Bonus Points	Total Points
										+	+	=

Lesson 77

Name _____ Date _____

Part A

1. _____
2. _____
3. _____
4. _____
5. _____

Part B

1. _____
2. _____
3. _____
4. _____
5. _____
6. _____
7. _____
8. _____

Part C

1. _____
2. _____
3. _____
4. _____

Name _____ Date _____

Part D

Circle the misspelled word in each group. Then write it correctly in the blank.

1. feature
   any
   poisonus
   fly

   _____

2. hopeful
   blissfull
   stopper
   friend

   _____

3. portabel
   rise
   herbal
   traps

   _____

4. lose
   fone
   passage
   shouldn't

   _____

5. rental
   work
   eqwip
   passive

   _____

6. reported
   finest
   retract
   disstract

   _____

7. lightly
   hotest
   catcher
   driest

   _____

8. hopefulnes
   about
   thoughtful
   furious

   _____

Part E

Draw a line from each word to its meaning.

cent   •   • an empty space

vary   •   • put words on paper

write •   • one hundred

whole •   • really

feat   •   • change

right •   • all parts together

very   •   • correct; opposite of left

hole   •   • something hard to do

PART	A	B	C	D	E	F	G	Worksheet Errors	Worksheet Points	Oral Points	Bonus Points	Total Points
										+	+	=

Lesson 78

Name _____ Date _____

Part A

1. _____   4. _____
2. _____   5. _____
3. _____

Part B

1. _____   3. _____
2. _____   4. _____

Part C

1. _____   5. _____
2. _____   6. _____
3. _____   7. _____
4. _____   8. _____

Part D

Write the contractions for the words in the first column.

	contraction		contraction
1. were not	= _____	3. we have	= _____
2. they will	= _____	4. did not	= _____

Part E

Add these morphographs together. Remember to use your spelling rules.

1. state + ing = _____   3. spin + er = _____

2. vise + ion = _____   4. heavy + est = _____

PART	A	B	C	D	E	F	G	Worksheet Errors	Worksheet Points	Oral Points	Bonus Points	Total Points
										+	+	=

Lesson 79

Name _____ Date _____

Part A

1. _____

_____

2. _____

_____

Part B

1. _____   3. _____

2. _____   4. _____

5. _____

Part C

Fill in the blanks to show the morphographs in each word.

1. _____ = question

2. _____ = breathless

3. _____ = resigned

4. _____ = revise

5. _____ = vision

Part D

Complete each sentence correctly with one of these words:

sent   cent   tail   feet   feat   tale

1. We saw an old jet plane with an orange ball on its _____ .

2. Don't spend one _____ more than you have to for copies.

3. After a long hike in the mountains, my _____ are usually sore for a week.

PART	A	B	C	D	E	F	G	Worksheet Errors	Worksheet Points	Oral Points	Bonus Points	Total Points
										+	+	=

Lesson 80

Name _____ Date _____

Part A

1. _____   4. _____

2. _____   5. _____

3. _____   6. _____

Part B

**These words are in the puzzle.
Circle 7 or more of the words.**

fact	know	wrap
diet	chief	heroic
win	fly	detect
tin	niece	reject

```
k  t  n  k  n  o  w
f  r  i  d  c  w  r
d  a  e  n  h  i  a
k  i  c  j  i  n  p
n  d  e  t  e  c  t
f  l  y  t  f  c  y
h  e  r  o  i  c  t
```

Part C

Draw a line from each word to its meaning.

sent •   • change

plain •   • all parts together

cent •   • something hard to do

tail •   • one hundred

vary •   • moved somewhere

right •   • simple; ordinary

feat •   • the end

whole •   • correct; opposite of left

Name _____ Date _____

Part **D**

Circle the misspelled word in each group.
Then write it correctly in the blank.

1. racing
   friendlyness
   helpful
   buzzy
   _____

2. boxs
   fits
   staying
   naming
   _____

3. hoping
   raging
   easey
   serve
   _____

4. poisonous
   civilly
   changer
   bigest
   _____

5. caged
   stepping
   berrys
   fittest
   _____

6. taken
   feeture
   grandest
   notable
   _____

7. sprayyer
   various
   remove
   couldn't
   _____

8. paused
   growing
   replace
   wonderring
   _____

PART	A	B	C	D	E	F	G	Worksheet Errors	Worksheet Points	Oral Points	Bonus Points	Total Points
									+	+	=	

Lesson 81

Name _____ Date _____

Part A

1. _____ 4. _____
2. _____ 5. _____
3. _____ 6. _____

Part B

1. _____ 4. _____
2. _____ 5. _____
3. _____ 6. _____

Part C

1. _____

_____

2. _____

_____

Part D

Fill in the blanks to show the morphographs in each word.

1. _____ = questionable

2. _____ = thirsty

3. _____ = explained

4. _____ = failure

Part E

Look at the last three letters of each word. Circle each short word that ends **cvc.**

1. poison   4. about

2. ship   5. joy

3. know   6. civil

PART	A	B	C	D	E	F	G	Worksheet Errors	Worksheet Points	Oral Points	Bonus Points	Total Points
										+	+	=

Lesson 82

Name _____ Date _____

Part A

I thoght my brothor woold photograf
our neice.

The vet gave the puppy an ingection to
prevent rabies.

_____

_____

_____

_____

_____

_____

_____

_____

Part B

1. _____   5. _____

2. _____   6. _____

3. _____   7. _____

4. _____   8. _____

Part C

1. _____   4. _____

2. _____   5. _____

3. _____   6. _____

Name _____ Date _____

Part D

Complete each sentence correctly with one of these words:

right   various   sent   tail

1. I _____ away for a book, but it never came.

2. Martin's desk is always cluttered with _____ things.

3. Ellen must have said the _____ thing because she did get the job.

4. Lee made a _____ out of rags for her kite.

5. Jill got more answers _____ than Jack did.

Part E

Figure out the rules and write them. Remember to spell the words correctly.

1. word when the word ends with a . . . with anything except **i** . . . change the **y** to **i** in a . . . **consonant-and-y** and . . . the next morphograph begins

_____

_____

2. vowel letter . . . next morphograph begins with a . . . from a word when the . . . drop the **final e**

_____

_____

PART	A	B	C	D	E	F	G	Worksheet Errors	Worksheet Points	Oral Points	Bonus Points	Total Points
										+	+	=

Lesson 84

Name _____ Date _____

Part A

1. _____   4. _____
2. _____   5. _____
3. _____   6. _____

Part B

1. _____   4. _____
2. _____   5. _____
3. _____   6. _____

Part C

1. _____   5. _____
2. _____   6. _____
3. _____   7. _____
4. _____   8. _____

Part D

Draw a line from each word to its meaning.

tail   •   • body parts

tale   •   • correct; opposite of left

sent   •   • something hard to do

cent   •   • a story

feat   •   • the end

feet   •   • moved somewhere

whole   •   • one hundred

right   •   • all parts together

Name _____ Date _____

Part E

Fill in the blanks to show the morphographs in each word.
Write the morphographs with plus signs between them.

1. _____ = recover

2. _____ = explain

3. _____ = preserved

4. _____ = hopping

5. _____ = hoping

6. _____ = business

7. _____ = cloudy

8. _____ = easy

9. _____ = relative

10. _____ = retraction

11. _____ = propel

12. _____ = retained

13. _____ = reducing

14. _____ = wrapper

15. _____ = famous

PART	A	B	C	D	E	F	G	Worksheet Errors	Worksheet Points	Oral Points	Bonus Points	Total Points
										+	+	=

Lesson 85

Name _____ Date _____

Part A

1. _____ 2. _____ 3. _____

Part B

1. _____ 5. _____

2. _____ 6. _____

3. _____ 7. _____

4. _____ 8. _____

Part C

1. _____ 4. _____

2. _____ 5. _____

3. _____ 6. _____

Part D

Fill in the blanks to show the morphographs in each word.
Write the morphographs with plus signs between them.

1. _____ = extent

2. _____ = failure

3. _____ = business

4. _____ = content

5. _____ = contract

6. _____ = glorious

7. _____ = studious

8. _____ = extract

Name _____ Date _____

Part E

Circle the misspelled word in each group. Then write it correctly in the blank.

1. hyuman

   carelessness

   hopeful

   rental

   _____

2. discoverer

   safeer

   whose

   you've

   _____

3. ll'l

   neatest

   income

   displease

   _____

4. active

   misplace

   rezerve

   deport

   _____

5. denying

   clannish

   fanciness

   namible

   _____

6. straghtest

   profuse

   edition

   equally

   _____

7. pause

   resort

   pasive

   defeat

   _____

8. babied

   lonly

   throwing

   proving

   _____

PART	A	B	C	D	E	F	G	Worksheet Errors	Worksheet Points	Oral Points	Bonus Points	Total Points
										+	+	=

Lesson 86

Name _____ Date _____

Part A

1. _____
2. _____
3. _____

4. _____
5. _____

Part B

1. _____
2. _____
3. _____
4. _____
5. _____

6. _____
7. _____
8. _____
9. _____
10. _____

Part C

Name _____ Date _____

Part D

Write contractions for the words in the first column.

contraction			contraction

1. are not   = _____   5. she will   = _____

2. we have   = _____   6. were not   = _____

3. does not   = _____   7. they are   = _____

4. could not = _____   8. they have = _____

Part E

Add these morphographs together. Remember to use your spelling rules.

1. chance + es   = _____

2. ship + er   = _____

3. thirst + y + ly   = _____

4. re + duce + ing   = _____

5. verse + ion   = _____

6. trans + fer   = _____

7. re + pel   = _____

8. heavy + est   = _____

9. in + cure + able   = _____

10. dis + ease   = _____

PART	A	B	C	D	E	F	G	Worksheet Errors	Worksheet Points	Oral Points	Bonus Points	Total Points
										+	+	=

Lesson 87

Name _____ Date _____

Part A

1. _____   5. _____
2. _____   6. _____
3. _____   7. _____
4. _____   8. _____

Part B

1. _____

_____

2. _____

_____

Part C

1. _____   5. _____
2. _____   6. _____
3. _____   7. _____
4. _____   8. _____

Part D

Add the morphographs together. Remember to use your rule.

1. show + en   = _____
2. length + en   = _____
3. blow + en   = _____
4. sew + en   = _____
5. prove + en   = _____
6. know + en   = _____
7. light + en   = _____

Name _____   Date _____

Part E

Draw a line from each word to its meaning.

sent •   • to make clothes

right •   • a thing that flies

tail •   • simple; ordinary

sew •   • a story

cent •   • the end

whole •   • one hundred

write •   • moved somewhere

feat •   • something hard to do

hole •   • body parts

plane •   • correct; opposite of left

tale •   • put words on paper

plain •   • all parts together

feet •   • an empty space

PART	A	B	C	D	E	F	G	Worksheet Errors	Worksheet Points	Oral Points	Bonus Points	Total Points
										+	+	=

Lesson 88

Name _____ Date _____

Part A

1. _____ 4. _____

2. _____ 5. _____

3. _____ 6. _____

Part B

1. _____ 5. _____

2. _____ 6. _____

3. _____ 7. _____

4. _____ 8. _____

Part C

Add these morphographs together. Remember to use your rule.

1. strength + en = _____

2. grow + en = _____

3. straight + en = _____

4. wide + en = _____

5. blow + en = _____

6. know + en = _____

7. mad + en = _____

8. throw + en = _____

Name _____ Date _____

Part D

Circle the misspelled word in each group. Then write it correctly on the line.

1. qwart

   revision

   thirsty

   failure

   _____

2. basic

   quoteable

   dangerous

   reverse

   _____

3. breifly

   physical

   spinning

   scope

   _____

4. transplant

   photograph

   straight

   heavyness

   _____

5. requested

   thousand

   breth

   duties

   _____

6. worried

   showen

   cloudy

   pleasure

   _____

Part E

Make 11 real words from the morphographs in the box.

serve	con	fine	de	form	re	train

1. _____   7. _____

2. _____   8. _____

3. _____   9. _____

4. _____   10. _____

5. _____   11. _____

6. _____

PART	A	B	C	D	E	F	G	Worksheet Errors	Worksheet Points	Oral Points	Bonus Points	Total Points
										+	+	=

Lesson **89**

Name _____ Date _____

Part Ⓐ

1. _____   4. _____

2. _____   5. _____

3. _____

Part Ⓑ

1. _____   5. _____

2. _____   6. _____

3. _____   7. _____

4. _____   8. _____

Part Ⓒ

Add these morphographs together. Remember to use your rule.

1. blow + ing   = _____

2. blow + en   = _____

3. fresh + en   = _____

4. sew + en   = _____

5. sew + ed   = _____

6. length + en   = _____

7. grow + en   = _____

8. throw + ing   = _____

Name _____ Date _____

Part D

Write **s** or **es** in the second column. Then add the morphographs together.

	s or es	new word		s or es	new word
1. class	+ _____	= _____	4. vary	+ _____	= _____
2. danger	+ _____	= _____	5. box	+ _____	= _____
3. progress	+ _____	= _____	6. story	+ _____	= _____

Part E

Fill in the blanks to show the morphographs in each word.
Write the morphographs with plus signs between them.

1. _____ = reverse
2. _____ = version
3. _____ = revise
4. _____ = revision
5. _____ = injection
6. _____ = prefolded
7. _____ = formal
8. _____ = physical
9. _____ = cubic
10. _____ = cutest

PART	A	B	C	D	E	F	G	Worksheet Errors	Worksheet Points	Oral Points	Bonus Points	Total Points
										+	+	=

Name _____ Date _____

Part A

1. _____   4. _____

2. _____   5. _____

3. _____   6. _____

Part B

1. _____   4. _____

2. _____   5. _____

3. _____   6. _____

Part C

1. _____   3. _____

2. _____   4. _____

Part D

Circle the short cvc morphographs.

1. ship   3. fer   5. box   7. gress   9. slow   11. sew

2. tect   4. boy   6. pel   8. cover   10. shed   12. star

Part E

Complete each sentence correctly with one of these words:

right   plainly   various   tailing

1. I could understand you better if you would speak more _____ .

2. Unfortunately, he said the _____ thing, but at the wrong time.

3. Mr. Penn awarded points to _____ students in his class.

PART	A	B	C	D	E	F	G	Worksheet Errors	Worksheet Points	Oral Points	Bonus Points	Total Points
										+	+	=

Lesson 91

Name _____ Date _____

Part A

1. _____ 4. _____

2. _____ 5. _____

3. _____ 6. _____

Part B

Underline any word that is misspelled and write it correctly in the right-hand column.

Some boyes were plaing a frendly game
of chanse.

_____

Janie took a quik breth and lifted the
heavie boxes.

_____

_____

_____

_____

_____

_____

_____

Part C

Add the morphographs together. Remember to use your spelling rules.

1. sew + en   = _____ 9. trans + fuse + ion   = _____

2. danger + ous   = _____ 10. un + fashion + able = _____

3. thirst + y + ness = _____ 11. con + verse + ion   = _____

4. big + est   = _____ 12. re + cover + able   = _____

5. lone + ly + ness = _____ 13. pro + vise + ion   = _____

6. cube + ic   = _____ 14. ex + pel   = _____

7. in + struct + ive + ly = _____ 15. dis + please + ure = _____

8. trans + fuse   = _____

Name _____ Date _____

Part **D**

**These words are in the puzzle.
Circle 7 or more of the words.**

shake	athlete	thousand
transact	scope	friend
seed	under	equal
voice	niece	farm

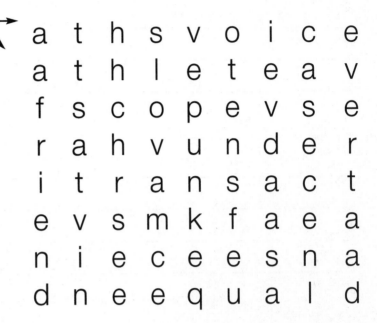

```
a t h s v o i c e
a t h l e t e a v
f s c o p e v s e
r a h v u n d e r
i t r a n s a c t
e v s m k f a e a
n i e c e e s n a
d n e e q u a l d
```

PART	A	B	C	D	E	F	G	Worksheet Errors	Worksheet Points	Oral Points	Bonus Points	Total Points
										+	+	=

Lesson 93

Name _____ Date _____

Part A

1. _____   4. _____

2. _____   5. _____

3. _____   6. _____

Part B

1. _____   5. _____

2. _____   6. _____

3. _____   7. _____

4. _____   8 _____

Part C

1. _____   5. _____

2. _____   6. _____

3. _____   7. _____

4. _____   8 _____

Part D

Underline any word that is misspelled and write it correctly in the right-hand column.

An unknoen athelete defeated a
famus runner.   _____

                                       _____

I have progresed wonderfully in my
photagraphy class.   _____

                                       _____

                                       _____

                                       _____

                                       _____

Name _____ Date _____

Part E

Fill in the blanks to show the morphographs in each word.
Write the morphographs with plus signs between them.

1. _____ = objection
2. _____ = revise
3. _____ = vision
4. _____ = version
5. _____ = destructively
6. _____ = conversion
7. _____ = athletic
8. _____ = shaken
9. _____ = constructive
10. _____ = fashionable
11. _____ = basics
12. _____ = exception

PART	A	B	C	D	E	F	G	Worksheet Errors	Worksheet Points	Oral Points	Bonus Points	Total Points
										+	+	=

Lesson 94

Name _____ Date _____

Part A

1. _____ 4. _____

2. _____ 5. _____

3. _____ 6. _____

Part B

1. _____ 4. _____

2. _____ 5. _____

3. _____ 6. _____

Part C

Add these morphographs together. Remember to use your spelling rules.

1. ob + struct = _____

2. happy + ly = _____

3. trans + gress + ion = _____

4. muse + ic + al = _____

5. un + fashion + able = _____

6. re + fer = _____

7. settle + ment = _____

8. athlete + ic = _____

9. know + en = _____

10. mis + con + cept + ion = _____

11. physic + ist = _____

12. ship + ment = _____

Name _____ Date _____

Part D

Circle the misspelled word in each group. Then write it correctly in the blank.

1. basic

   forgett

   transfusion

   distract

   _____

2. produce

   destruktive

   obtain

   deception

   _____

3. contract

   objective

   confuse

   transfir

   _____

4. reduse

   injecting

   regress

   content

   _____

5. dangerus

   repel

   contract

   graphic

   _____

Part E

**Make 4 real words from the morphographs in the box.
Be careful. Only four real words are possible.**

| re | mis | dis | pel | spell |

1. _____   3. _____

2. _____   4. _____

PART	A	B	C	D	E	F	G	Worksheet Errors	Worksheet Points	Oral Points	Bonus Points	Total Points
										+	+	=

Lesson 95

Name _____ Date _____

Part A

1. _____   5. _____

2. _____   6. _____

3. _____   7. _____

4. _____

Part B

Add these morphographs together. Remember your spelling rules.

1. real + ly   = _____   5. sure + ly   = _____

2. hopeful + ly   = _____   6. basic + ly   = _____

3. magic + ly   = _____   7. classic + ly = _____

4. flat + ly   = _____   8. equal + ly   = _____

Part C

Add these morphographs together. Remember your spelling rules.

1. settle + ment   = _____

2. verse + ion   = _____

3. con + struct + ion   = _____

4. re + fer   = _____

5. re + duce + ing   = _____

6. re + pel   = _____

7. con + tain + er   = _____

8. pro + ject + ed   = _____

9. muse + ic   = _____

10. ease + y   = _____

Name _____ Date _____

Part D

Draw a line from each word to its meaning.

son •   • to plant

four •   • the end

sow •   • a thing that flies

sew •   • a male child

plane •   • put words on paper

tale •   • one hundred

sent •   • a story

whole •   • all parts together

tail •   • to make clothes

cent •   • moved somewhere

write •   • the number 4

Part E

Fill in the blanks to show the morphographs in each word.
Write the morphographs with plus signs between them.

1. _____ = quarter

2. _____ = devise

3. _____ = thirsty

4. _____ = requesting

5. _____ = progressively

6. _____ = reverse

PART	A	B	C	D	E	F	G	Worksheet Errors	Worksheet Points	Oral Points	Bonus Points	Total Points
									+	+	=	

Lesson 96

Name _____ Date _____

Part A

1. _____   4. _____

2. _____   5. _____

3. _____   6. _____

Part B

Add the morphographs together. Remember the spelling rules.

1. cute + ly   = _____   5. logic + ly   = _____

2. physic + ly   = _____   6. gainful + ly = _____

3. faint + ly   = _____   7. quick + ly   = _____

4. heavy + ly   = _____   8. heroic + ly   = _____

Part C

Add these morphographs together. Remember the spelling rules.

1. pro + pel   = _____

2. in + fect + ion   = _____

3. in + struct + ion   = _____

4. ob + struct   = _____

5. ob + ject   = _____

6. de + fect + ive   = _____

7. con + fer   = _____

8. trans + fer   = _____

9. heavy + ness   = _____

10. for + give + ing   = _____

11. quest + ion + able = _____

12. athlete + ic   = _____

Name _____ Date _____

Part D

Figure out the rules and write them.

1. a word when the word ends with a . . . the next morphograph begins . . . change the **y** to **i** in . . . with anything except **i** . . . **consonant-and-y** and

   _____

   _____

2. next morphograph begins with **v** . . . word ends **cvc** and the . . . in a short word when the . . . double the final **c**

   _____

   _____

Part E

Circle the short cvc morphographs.

1. wander   4. fect   7. hop   10. tain

2. shed   5. bar   8. ship   11. pel

3. sew   6. bit   9. fer   12. poison

PART	A	B	C	D	E	F	G	Worksheet Errors	Worksheet Points	Oral Points	Bonus Points	Total Points
										+	+	=

Lesson 97

Name _____ Date _____

Part A

1. _____   4. _____

2. _____   5. _____

3. _____   6. _____

Part B

Add these morphographs together. Remember to use the rule about adding **al** before **ly**.

1. live + ly   = _____

2. graphic + ly   = _____

3. friendly + ness = _____

4. base + ment   = _____

5. transform + er   = _____

6. chief + ly   = _____

7. artistic + ly   = _____

8. glory + ous   = _____

Part C

1. _____   5. _____

2. _____   6. _____

3. _____   7. _____

4. _____   8. _____

Name _____ Date _____

Part D

Write **s** or **es** in the second column. Then add the morphographs together.

	s or **es**	**new word**		**s** or **es**	**new word**
1. reason	+ _____	= _____	5. box	+ _____	= _____
2. class	+ _____	= _____	6. copy	+ _____	= _____
3. brush	+ _____	= _____	7. fashion	+ _____	= _____
4. baby	+ _____	= _____	8. rich	+ _____	= _____

Part E

Fill in the blanks to show the morphographs in each word.
Write the morphographs with plus signs between them.

1. _____ = courting

2. _____ = living

3. _____ = basement

4. _____ = cubic

5. _____ = contend

6. _____ = pertain

7. _____ = compression

8. _____ = around

9. _____ = apart

10. _____ = transaction

PART	A	B	C	D	E	F	G	Worksheet Errors	Worksheet Points	Oral Points	Bonus Points	Total Points
										+	+	=

Lesson 98

Name _____ Date _____

Part Ⓐ

1. _____   4. _____

2. _____   5. _____

3. _____   6. _____

Part Ⓑ

1. _____   5. _____

2. _____   6. _____

3. _____   7. _____

4. _____   8. _____

Part Ⓒ

Add these morphographs together. Remember to use the rule about adding **al** before **ly.**

1. ship + ment   = _____

2. observe + ing   = _____

3. classic + ly   = _____

4. bid + ing   = _____

5. profuse + ly   = _____

6. basic + ly   = _____

7. detect + ion   = _____

8. define + ing   = _____

Name _____ Date _____

Part **D**

1. _____

_____

2. _____

_____

Part **E**

Circle the misspelled word in each group. Then write it correctly in the blank.

1. widely

   equaly

   unchanged

   strength

   _____

2. pushyness

   athletic

   heavily

   basic

   _____

3. thousand

   fashion

   version

   cheif

   _____

4. photograph

   vishun

   breathless

   spirit

   _____

5. rezerve

   dutiful

   request

   quoted

   _____

6. straight

   explain

   hopefully

   thrown

   _____

PART	A	B	C	D	E	F	G	Worksheet Errors	Worksheet Points	Oral Points	Bonus Points	Total Points
										+	+	=

Lesson 99

Name _____ Date _____

Part A

Study these words on your own. There will be a test on these words during your next spelling lesson.

dim   hid   star   rob   mud   grab   blot   bug   bed   leg

Part B

1. _____   5. _____

2. _____   6. _____

3. _____   7. _____

4. _____   8. _____

Part C

1. _____   4. _____

2. _____   5. _____

3. _____   6. _____

Part D

Add the morphographs together. Remember to use the rule about adding **al** before **ly.**

1. physic + ly   = _____   6. flat + ly   = _____

2. hopeful + ly = _____   7. thirst + y   = _____

3. live + ing   = _____   8. class + es   = _____

4. star + less   = _____   9. grab + ing   = _____

5. rob + er   = _____   10. mud + y   = _____

PART	A	B	C	D	E	F	G	Worksheet Errors	Worksheet Points	Oral Points	Bonus Points	Total Points
										+	+	=

Lesson 100

Name _____ Date _____

Part A

1. _____ 4. _____

2. _____ 5. _____

3. _____ 6. _____

Part B

1. _____ 6. _____

2. _____ 7. _____

3. _____ 8. _____

4. _____ 9. _____

5. _____ 10. _____

Part C

1. _____ 5. _____

2. _____ 6. _____

3. _____ 7. _____

4. _____ 8. _____

Name _____ Date _____

Part D

Add the morphographs together. Remember to use the rule about adding **al** before **ly.**

1. thousand + s = _____
2. quick + ly = _____
3. hop + er = _____
4. logic + ly = _____

5. forgetful + ly = _____
6. athletic + ly = _____
7. push + y = _____
8. run + ing = _____

Part E

Complete each sentence correctly with one of these words:

for   sewn   plainly   son   sow

1. Mr. Morgan's oldest _____ is a nurse.

2. The union members voted _____ the contract.

3. Several farmers _____ their wheat before winter.

4. All of Marcy's clothes are _____ by hand.

5. On a clear day, three mountains are _____ visible from Spencer's Creek.

6. The woman in the next apartment treats me like her own _____ .

PART	A	B	C	D	E	F	G	Worksheet Errors	Worksheet Points	Oral Points	Bonus Points	Total Points
										+	+	=

Name _____ Date _____

Part A

1. _____ 4. _____

2. _____ 5. _____

3. _____

Part B

	plural word			**plural word**
1. thief:	_____	3. loaf:	_____
2. wife:	_____	4. wolf:	_____

Part C

1. _____ 5. _____

2. _____ 6. _____

3. _____ 7. _____

4. _____ 8. _____

Part D

These words are in the puzzle.
Circle 9 or more of the words.

government	graphic	thousand
heroic	sort	tend
danger	wonder	spend
cement	alike	ground
shine	voters	

```
g t t w c s h i n e
g h t g o e p g t c
g o v e r n m e n t
r u c o n a d e n e
o s o r t d p e n d
u a l i k e r h r t
n n c c h e r o i c
d d a n g e r s m c
```

Name _____ Date _____

Part E

Fill in the blanks to show the morphographs in each word.

1. _____ = famous

2. _____ = exposure

3. _____ = structure

4. _____ = across

5. _____ = describe

6. _____ = infamous

7. _____ = texture

8. _____ = example

9. _____ = progressively

10. _____ = structural

11. _____ = factually

12. _____ = complain

13. _____ = perceptive

14. _____ = obstruction

15. _____ = around

PART	A	B	C	D	E	F	G	Worksheet Errors	Worksheet Points	Oral Points	Bonus Points	Total Points
										+	+	=

Lesson 103

Name _____ Date _____

Part A

1. _____   5. _____

2. _____   6. _____

3. _____   7. _____

4. _____   8. _____

Part B

plural word   **plural word**

1. wolf: _____   3. half: _____

2. wife: _____   4. shelf: _____

Part C

Write each of these words in a box. Write "free space" in one box.

across	infected	request	starry	govern
range	spirit	describe	recover	speechless
settle	sleepless	pretend	reasonable	thief

Name _____ Date _____

Part **D**

Make 11 real words from the morphographs in the box.

ob	ed	ject	pro	ion	in	de

1. _____   7. _____

2. _____   8. _____

3. _____   9. _____

4. _____   10. _____

5. _____   11. _____

6. _____

PART	A	B	C	D	E	F	G	Worksheet Errors	Worksheet Points	Oral Points	Bonus Points	Total Points
										+	+	=

Lesson 104

Name _____ Date _____

Part A

1. _____

_____

2. _____

_____

Part B

	plural word			plural word
1. shelf:	_____	3. calf:		_____
2. loaf:	_____	4. thief:		_____

Part C

1. _____   4. _____

2. _____   5. _____

3. _____   6. _____

Part D

Circle the short **cvc** morphographs.

1. grab	4. cur	7. mud	10. pel	13. state
2. mit	5. tend	8. fer	11. ship	14. shed
3. long	6. reason	9. coat	12. poison	15. logic

Name _____ Date _____

Part E

Fill in the blanks to show the morphographs in each word.

1. _____ = factual

2. _____ = unusual

3. _____ = alike

4. _____ = living

5. _____ = muddy

6. _____ = vision

7. _____ = visual

8. _____ = confinement

9. _____ = transaction

10. _____ = pushiness

PART	A	B	C	D	E	F	G	Worksheet Errors	Worksheet Points	Oral Points	Bonus Points	Total Points
										+	+	=

Name _____ Date _____

Part A

1. _____   5. _____
2. _____   6. _____
3. _____   7. _____
4. _____   8. _____

Part B

1. _____   4. _____
2. _____   5. _____
3. _____   6. _____

Part C

1. basic + ly   = _____
2. impose + ing   = _____
3. love + ly   = _____
4. athletic + ly   = _____
5. critic + ly   = _____
6. faint + ly   = _____

Name _____ Date _____

Part D

Draw a line from each word to its meaning.

son •   • one hundred

four •   • in favor of

sew •   • to plant

for •   • to make clothes

sow •   • the end

tale •   • a male child

tail •   • simple; ordinary

plain •   • the number 4

cent •   • a story

sent •   • moved somewhere

Part E

Add the morphographs together.

1. mud + y   = _____

2. easy + y + ly   = _____

3. lone + ly + ness = _____

4. dim + ly   = _____

5. choose + ing   = _____

6. type + ic + al   = _____

7. re + late + ive   = _____

8. vise + ual + ly   = _____

PART	A	B	C	D	E	F	G	Worksheet Errors	Worksheet Points	Oral Points	Bonus Points	Total Points
										+	+	=

Lesson 106

Name _____ Date _____

Part A

1. _____   5. _____

2. _____   6. _____

3. _____   7. _____

4. _____   8. _____

Part B

1. grow + en   = _____   5. straight + en   = _____

2. sweet + en   = _____   6. bit + en   = _____

3. act + ual   = _____   7. sew + en   = _____

4. blow + en   = _____   8. know + ing   = _____

Part C

1. _____   4. _____

2. _____   5. _____

3. _____   6. _____

Part D

Write the plural for each word. Remember to say the plural word to yourself.

1. calf: _____   3. shelf: _____

2. life: _____   4. wolf: _____

Name _____ Date _____

Part E

Complete each sentence correctly with one of these words:

tales   sent   four   plain   sew

1. John can _____ better than his sister Lil.

2. My father used to read us fairy _____ at bedtime.

3. Sue likes her tea with cream and sugar. I like mine _____ .

4. I have to _____ a button onto my coat before I can go out.

5. Jenny's uncle _____ her a fishing rod for her birthday.

6. A box has _____ sides, a top, and a bottom.

PART	A	B	C	D	E	F	G	Worksheet Errors	Worksheet Points	Oral Points	Bonus Points	Total Points
										+	+	=

Lesson 107

Name _____ Date _____

Part A

1. _____   4. _____

2. _____   5. _____

3. _____   6. _____

Part B

Study these words on your own. There will be a test on these words during your next spelling lesson.

| hit | spot | frog | rat | chin |
| trip | ton | run | net | pig |

Part C

1. _____   5. _____

2. _____   6. _____

3. _____   7. _____

4. _____   8. _____

Part D

1. _____   5. _____

2. _____   6. _____

3. _____   7. _____

4. _____   8. _____

Part E

Write the plural for each word. Remember to say the plural word to yourself.

1. knife: _____   3. life: _____

2. loaf: _____   4. self: _____

Name _____ Date _____

Part F

Fill in the blanks to show the morphographs in each word.

1. _____ = describe

2. _____ = around

3. _____ = ascribe

4. _____ = belong

5. _____ = prevent

6. _____ = invention

7. _____ = converge

8. _____ = critical

9. _____ = permit

10. _____ = defective

PART	A	B	C	D	E	F	G	Worksheet Errors	Worksheet Points	Oral Points	Bonus Points	Total Points
										+	+	=

Lesson 108

Name _____ Date _____

Part A

1. _____ 4. _____
2. _____ 5. _____
3. _____ 6. _____

Part B

1. _____ 6. _____
2. _____ 7. _____
3. _____ 8. _____
4. _____ 9. _____
5. _____ 10. _____

Part C

1. _____

_____

2. _____

_____

Name _____ Date _____

Part D

Write the plural for each word. Remember to say the plural word to yourself.

1. wife: _____   4. thief: _____

2. loaf: _____   5. self: _____

3. life: _____   6. wolf: _____

Part E

Add the morphographs together.

1. your + self   = _____   6. double + y   = _____

2. de + scribe + ing = _____   7. ob + ject + ive   = _____

3. pro + pose + ed   = _____   8. trans + act + ion = _____

4. room + y + ness   = _____   9. spot + ed   = _____

5. net + ed   = _____   10. con + sist   = _____

PART	A	B	C	D	E	F	G	Worksheet Errors	Worksheet Points	Oral Points	Bonus Points	Total Points
									+	+	=	

Name _____ Date _____

Part A

1. _____   4. _____

2. _____   5. _____

3. _____   6. _____

Part B

1. _____   5. _____

2. _____   6. _____

3. _____   7. _____

4. _____   8. _____

Part C

1. _____   4. _____

2. _____   5. _____

3. _____   6. _____

Part D

Circle the misspelled word in each group. Then write it correctly on the line.

1. magic
   fashun
   shedding
   thieves

   _____

2. athalete
   thousands
   retain
   instructive

   _____

3. statement
   recover
   cheifly
   version

   _____

4. consept
   reduce
   request
   fried

   _____

5. deceptive
   various
   heavily
   maddness

   _____

6. winner
   berries
   thrown
   basicly

   _____

Name _____ Date _____

Part E

Fill in the blanks to show the morphographs in each word.

1. _____ = subject

2. _____ = improvement

3. _____ = families

4. _____ = insisted

5. _____ = became

6. _____ = pretended

7. _____ = around

8. _____ = amusement

9. _____ = music

10. _____ = apartment

Part F

Figure out the rule and write it.

word ends **cvc** and the . . . in a short word when the . . . next morphograph begins with **v**
. . . double the final **c**

_____

_____

PART	A	B	C	D	E	F	G	Worksheet Errors	Worksheet Points	Oral Points	Bonus Points	Total Points
									+	+	=	

Lesson 110

Name _____   Date _____

February 2, 2007

Dear Hank,

   I got the pet lizard you cent me. Thank you vary much. Woold you believe that the little fellow has begun snaping at people? My aunt was plaing with the lizard last nite. Her fase was close to the little thing. All at once the lizard jumped up and bit her rite on the nose. Luckyly, the bite was not bad. She washed her face with plane water. She did'nt have a mark on her face, so you no the bite realy wasn't bad.

   Thanks again for the unuseual pet.

                    Your frend,

                    Emory

_____

_____

_____

_____

_____

_____

_____

_____

_____

_____

_____

_____

_____

_____

_____

_____

_____

PART	A	B	C	D	E	F	G	Worksheet Errors	Worksheet Points	Oral Points	Bonus Points	Total Points
									+	+	=	

Lesson 111

Name _____ Date _____

Part A

1. _____   5. _____

2. _____   6. _____

3. _____   7. _____

4. _____   8. _____

Part B

1. _____   6. _____

2. _____   7. _____

3. _____   8. _____

4. _____   9. _____

5. _____

Part C

Part D

Circle the short **cvc** morphographs.

1. run   4. fer   7. ject   10. wander

2. port   5. danger   8. snap   11. cur

3. bar   6. mit   9. shop   12. pel

Name _____ Date _____

Part E

Write the plural word. Remember to say the plural word to yourself.

plural word   **plural word**

1. knife: _____   5. thief: _____

2. wolf: _____   6. leaf: _____

3. life: _____   7. calf: _____

4. shelf: _____   8. wife: _____

Part F

Fill in the blanks to show the morphographs in each word.

1. _____ = refer

2. _____ = propel

3. _____ = commit

4. _____ = rerun

5. _____ = unsnap

6. _____ = concur

7. _____ = reinstate

8. _____ = families

PART	A	B	C	D	E	F	G	Worksheet Errors	Worksheet Points	Oral Points	Bonus Points	Total Points
										+	+	=

Lesson 112

Name _____ Date _____

Part A

1. chief: _____   3. gulf: _____

2. thief: _____   4. wolf: _____

Part B

1. _____   6. _____

2. _____   7. _____

3. _____   8. _____

4. _____   9. _____

5. _____

Part C

Circle the short cvc morphographs.

1. feet   3. chin   5. struct   7. fer   9. pel

2. mit   4. cur   6. critic   8. tain   10. trip

Name _____ Date _____

Part D

Circle the misspelled word in each group. Then write it correctly on the line.

1. personal

   basement

   before

   appart

   _____

2. perform

   obtain

   calf

   classicaly

   _____

3. briefs

   sobtract

   incur

   transmit

   _____

4. insist

   convert

   lively

   knifes

   _____

5. chooze

   grabbing

   womanhood

   danger

   _____

6. compound

   gradual

   defekt

   impression

   _____

PART	A	B	C	D	E	F	G	Worksheet Errors	Worksheet Points	Oral Points	Bonus Points	Total Points
										+	+	=

Lesson 113

Name _____ Date _____

Part A

1. _____   4. _____
2. _____   5. _____
3. _____

Part B

Study these words on your own. There will be a test on these words during your next spelling lesson.

red	bud	gas	top	hog
gum	pan	cut	car	

Part C

1. _____   4. _____
2. _____   5. _____
3. _____   6. _____

Part D

Fill in the blanks to show the morphographs in each word.

1. _____ = awhile
2. _____ = incurable
3. _____ = improve
4. _____ = subscribe
5. _____ = families
6. _____ = typical
7. _____ = subtracting
8. _____ = government
9. _____ = forceful
10. _____ = invert

Name _____ Date _____

Part E

Complete each sentence correctly with one of these words:

Sonny   week   plain   write   whole

1. Jill visits her grandparents every month. Carlos visits his every _____ .

2. Mr. Wilson is not my father, although he always calls me _____ .

3. Jim ate the _____ pie, and now he is sick.

4. I must remember to _____ a thank-you letter to my Aunt Chloe.

5. Just give me a _____ and simple answer. I don't want any fanciful tales.

6. Next _____ is Kim's birthday party. Are you coming?

7. Lui is only four years old, but he already knows how to read and _____ .

PART	A	B	C	D	E	F	G	Worksheet Errors	Worksheet Points	Oral Points	Bonus Points	Total Points
										+	+	=

Lesson 114

Name _____ Date _____

Part A

1. _____   3. _____

2. _____   4. _____

Part B

1. _____   6. _____

2. _____   7. _____

3. _____   8. _____

4. _____   9. _____

5. _____

Part C

1. puff: _____   3. half: _____

2. self: _____   4. chief: _____

Part D

Add the morphographs together.

1. cure + able   = _____   6. govern + ment = _____

2. im + pure   = _____   7. ex + ample+ s = _____

3. re + sub + mit = _____   8. reason + able = _____

4. e + vent + ual = _____   9. family + es   = _____

5. ad + just   = _____   10. ply + able   = _____

PART	A	B	C	D	E	F	G	Worksheet Errors	Worksheet Points	Oral Points	Bonus Points	Total Points
										+	+	=

Lesson 115

Name _____ Date _____

Part A

1. _____ 4. _____

2. _____ 5. _____

3. _____

Part B

1. _____ 4. _____

2. _____ 5. _____

3. _____ 6. _____

Part C

1. _____ 5. _____

2. _____ 6. _____

3. _____ 7. _____

4. _____ 8. _____

Part D

Write the plural for each word. Remember to say the plural word to yourself.

1. leaf: _____ 4. life: _____

2. calf: _____ 5. thief: _____

3. chief: _____ 6. safe: _____

Name _____ Date _____

Part E

Fill in the blanks to show the morphographs in each word.

1. _____ = incurable

2. _____ = typing

3. _____ = typical

4. _____ = reject

5. _____ = adjective

6. _____ = prevent

7. _____ = eventful

8. _____ = subscriber

9. _____ = department

10. _____ = glorious

PART	A	B	C	D	E	F	G	Worksheet Errors	Worksheet Points	Oral Points	Bonus Points	Total Points
										+	+	=

Lesson 116

Name _____ Date _____

Part A

1. _____   3. _____

2. _____

Part B

January 14, 2007

Dear Customer:

Are you spinding more time than you need to
on nasty household jobs? I'm righting to infrom
you that we are now produsing the most usefull
home appliance ever made. The new E-Z Home
Unit can do thousans of jobs in your home. It
changes the sheets on your family beds. It
replaces bad fuzes and protecs your house
from burglars. It will water any plants that you
have growing in your house. It also washs win-
dows, serves you dinner, and cures bad breth. It
comes packed in reuseable cardboard boxes.
The E-Z Home Unit can easyly be put together
using the helpfull instrucshuns that come with
each order.

   Please send us your order today.

                        Sincerely,

                        I.M. Selling

PART	A	B	C	D	E	F	G	Worksheet Errors	Worksheet Points	Oral Points	Bonus Points	Total Points
										+	+	=

Lesson 117

Name _____ Date _____

Part A

1. _____   3. _____

2. _____   4. _____

Part B

1. _____   4. _____

2. _____   5. _____

3. _____   6. _____

Part C

1. _____ = relentless

2. _____ = incomplete

3. _____ = surround

4. _____ = explore

Part D

Underline any word that is misspelled and write it correctly in the right-hand column.

A spoted frog solved the
magicle puzzel.   _____

The theif compoundded his troubles
by loosing his loot.   _____

_____

_____

_____

_____

_____

Name _____ Date _____

Part E

Add the morphographs together.

1. de + tect + ion   = _____

2. pro + tect + ion   = _____

3. re + act + ion   = _____

4. in + vent + ion   = _____

5. trans + gress + ion = _____

6. fact + ion + s   = _____

7. tract + ion   = _____

8. de + fect + ion   = _____

9. vise + ion   = _____

10. de + press + ion   = _____

PART	A	B	C	D	E	F	G	Worksheet Errors	Worksheet Points	Oral Points	Bonus Points	Total Points
										+	+	=

Name _____ Date _____

Part A

	ion form?	**or** or **er** form
1. fact:	_____	_____
2. design:	_____	_____
3. invent:	_____	_____
4. act:	_____	_____
5. speak:	_____	_____
6. photograph:	_____	_____

Part B

1. _____   4. _____

2. _____   5. _____

3. _____   6. _____

Part C

Circle the short **cvc** morphographs.

1. snap   3. mark   5. pel   7. critic   9. ceive

2. fer   4. ship   6. act   8. cur   10. box

Part D

Circle the misspelled word in each group. Then write it correctly on the line.

1. other	2. pityful	3. fashion	4. basicly
whose	wrong	thief	brought
civul	dangerous	reson	science
woman	uncover	knives	critic
_____	_____	_____	_____

Name _____ Date _____

Part E

Add the morphographs together.

1. sup + pose = _____

2. ex + plore + ing = _____

3. com + plete + ly = _____

4. sur + face = _____

5. pro + mote + ion = _____

6. re + lent + less = _____

7. ad + vise = _____

8. re + sume + ed = _____

9. un + e + vent + ful = _____

10. puzzle + ing = _____

PART	A	B	C	D	E	F	G	Worksheet Errors	Worksheet Points	Oral Points	Bonus Points	Total Points
										+	+	=

Lesson 119

Name _____ Date _____

Part A

1. _____ 2. _____ 3. _____

Part B

	ion form?	**or** or **er** form
1. transgress:	_____	_____
2. plant:	_____	_____
3. project:	_____	_____
4. compress:	_____	_____
5. retain:	_____	_____
6. tract:	_____	_____

Part C

1. rerun + ing = _____

2. infer + ing = _____

3. hit + er = _____

4. disarm + ed = _____

5. commit + ed = _____

6. ship + ing = _____

7. detect + ive = _____

8. snap + y = _____

Name _____ Date _____

Part D

Make 11 real words from the morphographs in the box.

ex	ion	press	re	im	ive	de

1. _____   7. _____

2. _____   8. _____

3. _____   9. _____

4. _____   10. _____

5. _____   11. _____

6. _____

Part E

1. in + sist + ing   = _____

2. ad + mit   = _____

3. pro + mote + ion   = _____

4. pre + sume   = _____

5. mot + ive   = _____

6. con + verse + ion   = _____

7. pre + vent + ion   = _____

8. un + re + solve + ed = _____

PART	A	B	C	D	E	F	G	Worksheet Errors	Worksheet Points	Oral Points	Bonus Points	Total Points
										+	+	=

Name _____ Date _____

Part Ⓐ

	ion form?	**or** or **er** form
1. revise:	_____	_____
2. light:	_____	_____
3. invent:	_____	_____
4. instruct:	_____	_____
5. stretch:	_____	_____
6. contract:	_____	_____

Part Ⓑ

Underline the morphograph that each word ends with. Then add the next morphograph.

1. admit + ed   = _____

2. dispel + ing   = _____

3. imbed + ing   = _____

4. instruct + ive   = _____

5. protect + ion   = _____

6. big + est   = _____

7. recur + ing   = _____

8. graph + ic   = _____

Part Ⓒ

1. _____ = profess

2. _____ = proceed

Name _____ Date _____

Part D

Underline any word that is misspelled and write it correctly in the right-hand column.

We weren't impresed with the
lengthy speech the athour gave.

_____

_____

The adventurors hopped to
discover hidden treasure,
but they faund nothing.

_____

_____

_____

_____

_____

_____

Part E

Fill in the blanks to show the morphographs in each word.

1. _____ = promotion

2. _____ = reviewing

3. _____ = dissolve

4. _____ = vision

5. _____ = confess

6. _____ = concise

7. _____ = exceedingly

8. _____ = predict

9. _____ = consume

10. _____ = section

PART	A	B	C	D	E	F	G	Worksheet Errors	Worksheet Points	Oral Points	Bonus Points	Total Points
										+	+	=

Lesson 121

Name _____ Date _____

Part A

1. _____ 4. _____

2. _____ 5. _____

3. _____

Part B

	ion form?	**or** or **er** form
1. heavy:	_____	_____
2. vise:	_____	_____
3. invent:	_____	_____
4. misspell:	_____	_____
5. confess:	_____	_____
6. inject:	_____	_____

Part C

1. _____ 5. _____

2. _____ 6. _____

3. _____ 7. _____

4. _____ 8. _____

Part D

Underline the morphograph that each word ends with. Then add the next morphograph.

1. repel + ing = _____ 5. submit + ing = _____

2. perfect +ion = _____ 6. spot + less = _____

3. remote + ly = _____ 7. compel + ing = _____

4. bliss + ful = _____ 8. commit + ment = _____

Name _____ Date _____

Part E

1. _____   4. _____

2. _____   5. _____

3. _____   6. _____

Part F

Add the morphographs together.

1. value + able   = _____

2. pre + dict + ion   = _____

3. de + sign + er   = _____

4. at + tract + ion   = _____

5. re + quest   = _____

6. quest + ion + able = _____

7. quiet + ly   = _____

8. at + tend + ed   = _____

9. di + vise + ion   = _____

10. sup + ply + es   = _____

PART	A	B	C	D	E	F	G	Worksheet Errors	Worksheet Points	Oral Points	Bonus Points	Total Points
									+	+	=	

Lesson 122

Name _____ Date _____

Part A

Study these words on your own. There will be a test on these words during Lesson 124.

set	up	pop	stir	sit
cap	fog	bat	tip	dig

Part B

1. _____
2. _____
3. _____
4. _____
5. _____
6. _____
7. _____
8. _____

Part C

If there is an **i-o-n** form of the word, write it in the second column.
If there is no **i-o-n** form, leave the second column blank.
In the last column, write the word with the morphograph **o-r** or **e-r.**

	ion form?	**or** or **er** form
1. vise:	_____	_____
2. profess:	_____	_____
3. review:	_____	_____
4. contract:	_____	_____
5. perform:	_____	_____
6. protect:	_____	_____

Name _____ Date _____

Part D

Underline the morphograph that each word ends with. Then add the next morphograph.

1. backpack + er = _____

2. joy + ous = _____

3. propel + ing = _____

4. emit + ing = _____

5. outfit + er = _____

6. refer + ed = _____

7. forget + ing = _____

8. unsnap + ed = _____

Part E

Fill in the blanks to show the morphographs in each word.

1. _____ = subverted

2. _____ = invert

3. _____ = conscience

4. _____ = exceed

5. _____ = implore

6. _____ = supported

7. _____ = reply

8. _____ = supplier

PART	A	B	C	D	E	F	G	Worksheet Errors	Worksheet Points	Oral Points	Bonus Points	Total Points
										+	+	=

Lesson 124

Name _____ Date _____

Part A

1. _____ 2. _____ 3. _____

Part B

1. _____ 6. _____

2. _____ 7. _____

3. _____ 8. _____

4. _____ 9. _____

5. _____ 10. _____

Part C

1. _____ = dismiss

2. _____ = record

3. _____ = appointment

Part D

Underline the morphograph that each word ends with. Then add the next morphograph.

1. spot + y   = _____

2. transfer + ing = _____

3. propel + er   = _____

4. unstop + able   = _____

5. overstep + ing = _____

6. commit + ment   = _____

Name _____ Date _____

Part E

Add the morphographs together.

1. dis + cord = _____

2. ex + plore + ing = _____

3. re + lent + less = _____

4. com + plete + ly = _____

5. sup + ply + es = _____

6. sur + face = _____

7. dict + ate + ion = _____

8. beauty + ful + ly = _____

9. pro + ceed + ing = _____

10. race + ial = _____

11. pre + cise + ion = _____

12. de + ceive + ed = _____

PART	A	B	C	D	E	F	G	Worksheet Errors	Worksheet Points	Oral Points	Bonus Points	Total Points
										+	+	=

Lesson 125

Name _____ Date _____

Part A

1. _____ 2. _____ 3. _____

Part B

1. _____ 5. _____ 8. _____

2. _____ 6. _____ 9. _____

3. _____ 7. _____ 10. _____

4. _____

Part C

November 19, 2007

Dear Mr. Swiss,

    We were glad to recieve your subscripshun to the Clock-of-the-Month-Club. Your furst clock owt to arrive within a weak. Each month, you will receive a new clock with a beautyful, original dezign. In the past, we have cent thouzunds of clocks that double as plantters, ships, wolfs, eyedroppers, and many other objecs.

    If you like the Clock-of-the-Month, keep it. We will bill you. If you do'nt like it, send it back in the original packege within fore days.

    Thank you for choozing the Clock-of-the-Month Club.

_____

_____

_____

_____

_____

_____

_____

_____

_____

_____

_____

_____

_____

PART	A	B	C	D	E	F	G	Worksheet Errors	Worksheet Points	Oral Points	Bonus Points	Total Points
										+	+	=

Name _____ Date _____

Part A

1. _____ 4. _____

2. _____ 5. _____

3. _____ 6. _____

Part B

1. _____ = concern

2. _____ = magician

3. _____ = direct

Part C

Circle the short **cvc** morphographs.

1. stir
2. sist
3. play

4. mit
5. cur
6. major

7. box
8. fer
9. ceive

10. cover
11. pel
12. spin

13. know
14. reason
15. trap

Part D

Draw a line from each word to its meaning.

week •   • correct; opposite of left

sew •   • a story

plain •   • happy

sent •   • to make clothes

tale •   • they own it

their •   • simple; ordinary

marry •   • not strong

right •   • moved somewhere

weak •   • to wed; unite

merry •   • seven days

Name _____ Date _____

Part E

Add the morphographs together.

1. part + ial + ly   = _____

2. di + vise + ion   = _____

3. ease + y   = _____

4. major + ite + y   = _____

5. con + fess + ion   = _____

6. in + com + plete   = _____

7. value + able   = _____

8. ad + ject + ive   = _____

9. govern + ment + al   = _____

10. pro + ceed   = _____

11. re + serve + ate + ion = _____

12. re + sign + ate + ion = _____

PART	A	B	C	D	E	F	G	Worksheet Errors	Worksheet Points	Oral Points	Bonus Points	Total Points
										+	+	=

Name _____ Date _____

Part A

1. water + ed   = _____   4. critic + al   = _____

2. mother + ly = _____   5. contain + er = _____

3. permit + ing = _____   6. cap + ed   = _____

Part B

June 30, 2007

Dear Sandy,

I realy like to recieve your letters. You always right about wonderrful advenchures. I had not knowen that there are poisonus snakes at the lake. I'll bet you were vary happy to return home.

I have been studing insects for a sciense project. Most people don't like insects, but I think many of them are actualy bueatiful. I have been keeping abowt a thousand of them in my bedroom.

As your firend, I must tell you about one weekness in your letters. Your speling is pityful. I can barely read haf the words. I hope you will try to make fewer misstakes in your next letter.

Yours sincerely,

Pat

PART	A	B	C	D	E	F	G	Worksheet Errors	Worksheet Points	Oral Points	Bonus Points	Total Points
									+	+	=	

Lesson 128

Name _____ Date _____

Part A

1. _____   3. _____

2. _____   4. _____

Part B

1. infer + ing   = _____   4. recur + ed   = _____

2. unstop + able = _____   5. spirit + ual = _____

3. uncover + ed = _____   6. stir + ing   = _____

Part C

Fill in the blanks to show the morphographs in each word.

1. _____ = valuable

2. _____ = rejection

3. _____ = eject

4. _____ = evaluate

5. _____ = concern

6. _____ = divide

7. _____ = direction

8. _____ = appoint

9. _____ = improvement

10. _____ = approval

11. _____ = around

12. _____ = noted

13. _____ = notable

14. _____ = record

15. _____ = prediction

Name _____ Date _____

Part D

These words are in the puzzle.
Circle 7 or more of the words.

receive	sect	settle
sure	serve	beauty
their	trouble	spotted
tension	double	taken
stir	week	

```
d  o  u  b  l  e  r
s  t  h  e  i  r  e
s  p  s  a  d  s  c
t  r  o  u  b  l  e
s  e  c  t  r  w  i
e  e  n  y  t  e  v
r  s  t  s  e  e  e
v  t  t  t  i  k  d
e  i  s  e  l  o  i
s  r  t  a  k  e  n
```

Part E

Add the morphographs together. Remember to use your spelling rules.

1. tense + ion = _____

2. pro + cess = _____

3. com + plete + ion = _____

4. con + dense + ate + ion = _____

5. beauty + ful + ly = _____

6. ad + verse + ite + y = _____

7. inter + cept + ion = _____

8. dig + ing = _____

9. ease + y + ly = _____

10. face + ial = _____

11. un + use + ual = _____

12. heavy + est = _____

PART	A	B	C	D	E	F	G	Worksheet Errors	Worksheet Points	Oral Points	Bonus Points	Total Points
										+	+	=

Lesson 129

Name _____ Date _____

Part A

1. expel + ing   = _____

2. poison + ous = _____

3. project + ion = _____

4. combat + ed = _____

5. wonder + ful = _____

6. dig + er   = _____

Part B

1. _____   5. _____

2. _____   6. _____

3. _____   7. _____

4. _____   8. _____

Part C

Fill in the blanks to show the morphographs in each word.

1. _____ = remote

2. _____ = active

3. _____ = motive

4. _____ = motivate

5. _____ = motivation

6. _____ = promotion

7. _____ = predict

8. _____ = dictate

9. _____ = dictation

10. _____ = densely

11. _____ = condense

12. _____ = condensation

Name _____ Date _____

Part D

Complete each sentence correctly with these words.

married   their   merry   marry   there   weekly

1. Everyone at the celebration was in a _____ mood.

2. Terry's sisters invest nearly all _____ money.

3. I think Louie will _____ an athlete someday.

4. My desk is by a window, but I don't like it _____ .

5. How long have your parents been _____ ?

6. The teachers are going to discuss the talent show at _____

_____ meeting.

Part E

If there is an i-o-n form of the word, write it in the second column.
If there is no i-o-n form, leave the second column blank.
In the last column, write the word with the morphograph o-r or e-r.

	ion form?	**or** or **er** form
1. direct:	_____	_____
2. inspect:	_____	_____
3. review:	_____	_____
4. dictate:	_____	_____
5. propel:	_____	_____
6. farm:	_____	_____

PART	A	B	C	D	E	F	G	Worksheet Errors	Worksheet Points	Oral Points	Bonus Points	Total Points
										+	+	=

Lesson 130

Name _____ Date _____

Part A

1. _____   3. _____

2. _____   4. _____

Part B

1. _____ + _____ = _____

2. _____ + _____ = _____

3. _____ + _____ = _____

4. _____ + _____ = _____

Part C

1. _____   5. _____

2. _____   6. _____

3. _____   7. _____

4. _____   8. _____

Part D

1. _____ = preparing

2. _____ = controlled

Name _____ Date _____

Part **E**

Fill in the blanks to show the morphographs in each word.

1. _____ = define

2. _____ = finite

3. _____ = infinite

4. _____ = infinity

5. _____ = commend

6. _____ = recommend

PART	A	B	C	D	E	F	G	Worksheet Errors	Worksheet Points	Oral Points	Bonus Points	Total Points
									+	+	=	

Lesson 131

Name _____ Date _____

Part A

1. _____ 3. _____

2. _____ 4. _____

Part B

1. _____ = elect

2. _____ = perturb

Part C

1. _____ + _____ = _____

2. _____ + _____ = _____

3. _____ + _____ = _____

4. _____ + _____ = _____

Part D

Add the morphographs together.

1. con + stant + ly   = _____

2. pro + cess   = _____

3. in + di + rect   = _____

4. con + cern   = _____

5. pro + ceed + ing   = _____

6. re + pel   = _____

7. ideal + ly   = _____

8. grave + ite + y   = _____

9. tense + ion   = _____

10. e + value + ate + ion = _____

Name _____ Date _____

Part E

Circle the misspelled word in each group. Then write it correctly on the line.

1. nervous

    magicle

    dangerous

    critical

    _____

2. sciense

    majority

    shelves

    weren't

    _____

3. puzzling

    simple

    watch

    fancyest

    _____

4. container

    depression

    transport

    thoughtfullness

    _____

5. proclame

    human

    destructive

    reviewer

    _____

6. spoiled

    bilding

    reasonable

    berries

    _____

PART	A	B	C	D	E	F	G	Worksheet Errors	Worksheet Points	Oral Points	Bonus Points	Total Points
										+	+	=

Lesson 132

Name _____ Date _____

Part A

1. _____   5. _____

2. _____   6. _____

3. _____   7. _____

4. _____   8. _____

Part B

1. _____ = providing

2. _____ = beginner

Part C

1. _____ + _____ = _____

2. _____ + _____ = _____

3. _____ + _____ = _____

4. _____ + _____ = _____

Name _____ Date _____

Part Ⓓ

Add the morphographs together. Remember to use your spelling rules.

1. base + ic + ly = _____

2. medic + ly = _____

3. beauty + ful = _____

4. scarce + ite + y = _____

5. con + trol + ing = _____

6. per + mit + ed = _____

7. pro + fess + ion = _____

8. di + vise + ion = _____

9. pity + ful = _____

10. real + ize + ate + ion = _____

Part Ⓔ

Underline any word that is misspelled and write it correctly in the right-hand column.

Marty's family has a beautyful
home with a vue of the lake.

_____

I'm hopping for a good night's
sleep because I have to give a
speach tomorrow.

_____

_____

_____

_____

_____

_____

PART	A	B	C	D	E	F	G	Worksheet Errors	Worksheet Points	Oral Points	Bonus Points	Total Points
									+	+		=

Lesson 133

Name _____ Date _____

Part A

1. _____   3. _____

2. _____   4. _____

Part B

1. _____   5. _____

2. _____   6. _____

3. _____   7. _____

4. _____   8. _____

Part C

1. _____ + _____ = _____

2. _____ + _____ = _____

3. _____ + _____ = _____

4. _____ + _____ = _____

Part D

1. _____ = medicine

2. _____ = backward

Name _____ Date _____

Part E

Add the morphographs together.

1. se + pare + ate = _____

2. cave + ite + y = _____

3. real + ize + ate + ion = _____

4. in + di + rect + ly = _____

5. e + lect + ion = _____

6. part + ial + ly = _____

7. in + tense + ite + y = _____

8. sane + ite + ate + ion = _____

9. un + author + ized + ed = _____

10. se + lect + ion = _____

PART	A	B	C	D	E	F	G	Worksheet Errors	Worksheet Points	Oral Points	Bonus Points	Total Points
										+	+	=

Lesson 134

Name _____ Date _____

Part A

1. _____   2. _____   3. _____

Part B

1. _____   5. _____

2. _____   6. _____

3. _____   7. _____

4. _____   8. _____

Part C

1. _____   5. _____

2. _____   6. _____

3. _____   7. _____

4. _____   8. _____

Part D

1. _____ = forbidden

Name _____ Date _____

Part E

Fill in the blanks to show the morphographs in each word.

1. _____ = refine

2. _____ = prepare

3. _____ = finite

4. _____ = forward

5. _____ = preparation

6. _____ = separate

7. _____ = medical

8. _____ = separation

9. _____ = medicine

10. _____ = completely

PART	A	B	C	D	E	F	G	Worksheet Errors	Worksheet Points	Oral Points	Bonus Points	Total Points
										+	+	=

Name _____ Date _____

Part A

1. _____
2. _____
3. _____

Part B

1. _____ = forgotten
2. _____ = desirous

Part C

Add the morphographs together. Remember to use your spelling rules.

1. for + bid + en = _____
2. dis + miss + al = _____
3. un + con + trol + ed = _____
4. ac + cent + ed = _____
5. re + cur + ing = _____
6. real + ize + ate + ion = _____
7. beauty + ful + ly = _____
8. pro + pel + er = _____
9. com + mit + ment = _____
10. un + com + mit + ed = _____
11. grave + ite + y = _____
12. note + ice + ing = _____

Name _____ Date _____

Part D

Underline any word that is misspelled and write it correctly in the right-hand column.

We will autherize the contract for
the construshion of the medicle building.

_____

_____

The idealist was'nt vary reelistic
about planing her afternoon.

_____

_____

You can win most ellections with a
majoritee of the votes.

_____

_____

_____

_____

_____

_____

_____

Part E

If there is an i-o-n form of the word, write it in the second column.
If there is no i-o-n form, leave the second column blank.
In the last column, write the word with the morphograph o-r or e-r.

	ion form?	**or** or **er** form
1. collect:	_____	_____
2. supervise:	_____	_____
3. report:	_____	_____
4. profess:	_____	_____
5. dictate:	_____	_____
6. detect:	_____	_____

PART	A	B	C	D	E	F	G	Worksheet Errors	Worksheet Points	Oral Points	Bonus Points	Total Points
										+	+	=

Name _____ Date _____

Part A

1. _____ = sociable

2. _____ = exhilarate

Part B

1. _____ 2. _____

Part C

1. _____

_____

2. _____

_____

Part D

1. _____ 4. _____

2. _____ 5. _____

3. _____ 6. _____

Name _____ Date _____

Part E

Draw a line from each word to its meaning.

their •	• all parts together
marry •	• not strong
right •	• they own it
weak •	• put words on paper
there •	• to wed; unite
write •	• happy
plain •	• they are
whole •	• correct; opposite of left
merry •	• in that place
they're •	• simple; ordinary

PART	A	B	C	D	E	F	G	Worksheet Errors	Worksheet Points	Oral Points	Bonus Points	Total Points
										+	+	=

Name _____ Date _____

Part A

1. _____ 5. _____

2. _____ 6. _____

3. _____ 7. _____

4. _____ 8. _____

Part B

1. _____ 4. _____

2. _____ 5. _____

3. _____ 6. _____

Part C

Make 15 real words from the morphographs in the box.

un	ate	vent	ion	able	pre	dict	or	in

1. _____ 9. _____

2. _____ 10. _____

3. _____ 11. _____

4. _____ 12. _____

5. _____ 13. _____

6. _____ 14. _____

7. _____ 15. _____

8. _____

Name _____   Date _____

Part D

Fill in the blanks to show the morphographs in each word.

1. _____ = realization

2. _____ = decreasing

3. _____ = partially

4. _____ = designation

5. _____ = condensation

6. _____ = civilization

7. _____ = dismiss

8. _____ = admission

9. _____ = sociable

10. _____ = hilarity

Part E

Add the morphographs together.

1. in + quire + y   = _____   6. ap + ply + es   = _____

2. ex + hilar + ate = _____   7. at + tend + ed   = _____

3. magic + ian   = _____   8. sur + round + s = _____

4. un + dis + pute = _____   9. de + fine + ite   = _____

5. intro + duce   = _____   10. marry + age   = _____

PART	A	B	C	D	E	F	G	Worksheet Errors	Worksheet Points	Oral Points	Bonus Points	Total Points
										+	+	=

Lesson 138

Name _____ Date _____

Part A

1. _____   5. _____
2. _____   6. _____
3. _____   7. _____
4. _____   8. _____

Part B

1. _____   4. _____
2. _____   5. _____
3. _____   6. _____

Part C

Add the morphographs together. Remember to use your spelling rules.

1. base + ic + ly   = _____
2. grave + ite + y   = _____
3. be + gin + er   = _____
4. per + mit + ed   = _____
5. friend + ly + ness   = _____
6. di + vide   = _____
7. know + en   = _____
8. se + pare + ate + ion = _____
9. govern + ment + al   = _____
10. a + cross   = _____
11. athlete + ic + ly   = _____
12. vary + ous   = _____

Name _____ Date _____

Part D

Fill in the blanks to show the morphographs in each word.

1. _____ = permitting

2. _____ = refinement

3. _____ = finally

4. _____ = business

5. _____ = indefinite

6. _____ = expensive

7. _____ = accurate

8. _____ = incurable

Part E

Complete each sentence correctly with these words:

they're   right   their   there   write

1. Mark put my skateboard in the garage, but I didn't want it _____ .

2. After Lee and Tony's party, _____ going to clean the house themselves.

3. What do you call people who can _____ equally well with

   _____ left hand or _____ hand.

4. My dogs spread _____ toys all over the kitchen floor.

PART	A	B	C	D	E	F	G	Worksheet Errors	Worksheet Points	Oral Points	Bonus Points	Total Points
									+	+	=	

Lesson 139

Name _____ Date _____

Part A

1. _____   5. _____

2. _____   6. _____

3. _____   7. _____

4. _____   8. _____

Part B

Underline any word that is misspelled and write it correctly in the right-hand column.

The professer has a busness
that is seperate from her
teaching.

_____

_____

J.P. found inexpensuve transportation
for having his equipment transfered
to his new office.

_____

_____

_____

_____

_____

_____

_____

_____

Part C

Figure out the rules and write them.

1. from a word when the . . . vowel letter . . . drop the **final e** . . . next morphograph begins with a

_____

_____

2. and the next morphograph begins with anything . . . when the word ends with a **consonant-and-y** . . . except **i** . . . change the **y** to **i** in a word

_____

_____

Name _____   Date _____

Part **D**

Add the morphographs together.

1. image + ine   = _____

2. soci + al   = _____

3. nine + teen   = _____

4. civil + ize + ate + ion   = _____

5. un + fashion + able   = _____

6. image + ine + ate + ion   = _____

7. intro + duct + ion   = _____

8. dis + re + pute + able   = _____

9. muse + ic + ian   = _____

10. com + mend + able   = _____

11. inter + miss + ion   = _____

12. pro + verb + ial   = _____

PART	A	B	C	D	E	F	G	Worksheet Errors	Worksheet Points	Oral Points	Bonus Points	Total Points
										+	+	=

Section A

Bases introduced in Lessons 1–13

quiet	1	brush	2	take	6	human	8
fresh	1	spell	3	author	6	stretch	8
born	1	back	3	motor	6	catch	8
pack	1	thick	3	help	6	dull	8
wonder	1	happy	3	grand	7	press	9
spend	1	match	4	friend	7	form	9
light	2	port	4	sell	7		
crash	2	sort	4	fill	7		

Section B

Some words made from morphographs taught through Lesson 13

author	grand	motoring	selling
authoring	grandest	pack	sort
back	grandness	port	sorting
backless	happy	portable	spell
born	help	press	spelling
brush	helpless	quiet	spend
catch	helplessness	quietest	spendable
catching	human	quietness	stretch
crash	humanness	reborn	stretching
dull	light	refill	take
dullest	lightest	refillable	thick
dullness	lightness	reform	thickest
fill	match	refresh	thickness
filling	matching	refreshing	unborn
form	matchless	rematch	unhappy
forming	mismatch	repack	unpack
formless	misspell	report	unrefillable
fresh	misspending	repress	unrefreshing
freshest	mistake	resellable	wonder
friend	motor	sell	wondering

Appendix B

Section A

Bases introduced in Lessons 14–23

like	14	use	15	trace	17	equal	20
fine	14	rest	16	face	17	hate	20
name	14	dine	16	cent	17	farm	20
note	14	serve	16	snap	19	cart	20
right	15	care	16	mad	19	arm	20
night	15	bare	16	sad	19	bar	20
grade	15	bliss	17	swim	19		
wide	15	city	17	shop	19		
hope	15	rent	17	run	19		

Section B

Rules introduced in Lessons 14–23

Final-E Rule (Lesson 14) "When a word ends in **e** and you add a morphograph that begins with a vowel letter, drop the **e.**"

Section C

Some words made of morphographs taught through Lesson 23

arm	farm	misuse	rest	unpacked
armed	farmer	name	restlessly	unrented
armless	filler	nameless	restlessness	unrest
authored	fine	namely	retrace	unsnap
backer	finely	night	reuse	usable
backpacker	fineness	notable	right	use
bar	former	note	rightly	uselessness
bare	friendly	packer	run	wide
barely	grade	prepacked	sad	widely
bliss	grander	preserve	sadness	wondered
brushed	hate	prestretched	sadly	
care	hope	quietly	serve	
carelessly	hopelessly	recent	shop	
carelessness	humanly	refine	snap	
cart	lightly	reformed	stretchable	
carted	likable	refreshing	stretcher	
catcher	like	rematch	swim	
cent	likeness	rename	trace	
city	mad	rent	unequal	
dine	madness	renter	unequally	
equal	mismatched	reported	unfarmable	
equally	misspelled	repressed	unfriendly	
face	misspelling	rerun	ungraded	
faceless	mistake	reserve	unlikely	

Appendix C

Section A

Bases introduced in Lessons 24–35

race	24	stop	25	deal	28	world	30
force	24	wash	27	lone	28	step	30
choice	24	water	27	clan	28	drop	30
voice	24	want	27	sign	29	shine	30
coil	24	wander	27	length	29	play	32
plan	24	nerve	27	strength	29	boy	32
change	25	pass	27	hot	29	joy	32
page	25	verb	28	big	29	civil	32
rage	25	herb	28	lose	29	berry	32
cage	25	real	28	work	30		

Section B

Rules introduced in Lessons 24–35

Doubling Rule (Lesson 25) "When a short word ends **cvc** and the next morphograph bgins with a **v,** double the final **c.**"

Vowel-Consonant (Lesson 32) "**Y** at the end of a morphograph is a vowel letter. The vowels are **a, e, i, o, u,** and **y** at the end of a morphograph."

Section C

Some words made from morphographs taught through Lesson 35

barely	deal	forcefully	liked	plan	resign	uncaged	want
bareness	dealer	formal	likely	play	resigning	unchanging	wash
barest	defacing	freshener	liken	playful	rested	uncivil	washer
berry	defining	hateful	likeness	portable	restful	uncoiled	water
big	deform	hating	likening	prewashed	resting	undefinable	widely
blissful	degrade	helpfulness	liking	quietest	restless	unlikable	widen
boy	delighted	herb	lone	quietly	rightfully	unmistakable	wideness
boyish	delightful	herbal	lonely	quietness	shine	unnerving	widening
boyishness	denoting	hoped	lose	race	shining	unplayable	widest
cage	departed	hopeful	loser	racer	sign	unreal	work
cageless	depressing	hopeless	misstep	rage	signal	unreserved	workable
cared	deserved	hoping	mistaken	raging	signed	unwanted	worker
careful	designer	hot	nerve	real	signing	usable	world
careless	dining	hotter	notable	really	step	usage	worldly
caring	drop	hottest	noted	recoil	stop	used	wonderful
change	equip	human	noting	redealing	strength	useful	
choice	faced	joy	packaging	redefine	stretchable	using	
choicest	final	joyful	page	refinable	stretched	verb	
civil	finely	joyless	pageless	refreshen	stretching	verbally	
civilly	fineness	length	paging	renamed	taken	voice	
clan	finest	lengthening	pass	rental	taking	voicing	
coil	force	likable	passage	replay	thicken	wander	

Appendix D

Section A

Bases introduced in Lessons 36–46

study	36	sturdy	37	buzz	38	tax	40	story	42	rise	43
pity	36	fur	37	fuzz	38	try	41	safe	42	mother	43
copy	36	hurry	37	write	38	late	41	trap	42	brother	43
nasty	36	fuse	37	busy	40	fit	41	might	42	are	43
cry	36	baby	38	worry	40	should	41	she	42	were	43
dry	36	wrong	38	fox	40	would	41	have	42	does	43
fancy	37	wrap	38	box	40	could	41	carry	43		

Section B

Rules introduced in Lessons 36–46

Y-to-I Rule (Lesson 36) "Change the **y** to **i** when a word ends with a consonant-and-**y**, and the next morphograph begins with anything, except **i**."

Plural Variation (Lesson 38) "If a word ends in **s, z, sh,** or **ch,** you add **es** to make the plural."

Plural Variation (Lesson 41) "If a word ends in **s, z, sh, ch,** or **x,** you add **es** to make the plural. The letter **x** acts like two consonant letters."

Section C

Some words made from morphographs taught through Lesson 46

are	carefully	degrade	fur	lately	players	runner	stopper	unwrap
baby	careless	degrading	furs	later	plays	sadder	stopping	usage
babyish	carelessly	delight	fuse	lighter	presses	saddest	story	useful
backs	carry	delighting	fuzz	lighting	prewrap	sadly	stretched	usefully
baggage	carrying	deserve	grader	likeliest	raged	sadness	stretcher	useless
bagged	catches	deserving	grading	madder	recopy	safe	stretching	uselessly
bagging	changes	designers	happily	maddest	redefine	safely	study	user
bared	clannish	dined	happiness	madly	refusal	served	studying	using
barer	confined	diner	have	madness	refused	server	sturdy	washed
baring	confines	dining	having	might	related	serving	swimming	washer
barred	conform	does	hopeful	misfit	rented	she	tax	washing
bigger	confuse	dropper	hopefully	mother	renter	shop	taxed	were
biggest	confusing	dry	hopeless	motherless	renting	shopped	taxes	worlds
box	connote	drying	hopelessly	motors	resorts	shopping	thicker	worry
boxer	conserve	equals	hurry	nasty	rested	shops	thickest	worrying
boxes	consign	fancy	hurrying	package	restful	signs	thickly	would
boys	copy	finals	inborn	packaged	resting	should	thickness	wrap
brother	copiable	finer	inform	packaging	restless	snapped	trap	wrapper
brotherly	copying	fining	informally	packed	restlessly	snapper	trappers	write
brushes	could	fit	informer	packer	rests	snapping	trial	writing
busy	crashes	fitness	inhuman	packing	restudy	snaps	trying	wrong
busying	cry	fitting	instep	passages	rewrap	sorts	try	wrongly
buzz	crying	forms	intake	passes	rights	stepped	unequal	
buzzes	define	fox	joyful	pity	rise	stepping	unfit	
buzzers	defining	foxes	joys	pitying	rising	steps	uninformed	
careful	defuse	friendless	late	planning		stopped	unsturdy	

Section  A

Bases introduced in Lessons 47–56

stay	48	whether	49	loud	50	fact	53
deny	48	what	49	move	50	claim	53
did	48	when	49	woman	51	main	53
they	48	whole	50	cloud	51	file	53
fly	48	where	50	leave	51	vary	53
other	48	whose	50	neat	51	tract	53
come	49	sound	50	edit	51		
man	49	proud	50	act	53		

Section B

Rules introduced in Lessons 47–56

Contractions (Lesson 47) "A contraction is made from two words, and a contraction has a part missing. We show that the part is missing with an apostrophe."

Section C

Some words made from morphographs taught through Lesson 56

act	exacting	hateful	nastiest	shining	trapping
armless	exchanges	hater	nastily	shopped	trial
bliss	exclaim	hating	nastiness	shopper	unmoved
busiest	exports	he'll	neat	shopping	unrefillable
busier	express	hoped	neatly	signals	unsound
busily	extract	hopeful	other	signers	unstops
business	fact	hoping	packing	snapping	usable
carting	fancied	inexact	pitied	sound	user
civilly	fancier	invariable	pitiful	soundest	using
claim	fanciful	joyfully	pitying	soundly	variable
cloud	fancying	leave	played	soundness	varied
contraction	file	leaving	player	spell	vary
come	filing	lighter	playful	stay	varying
cried	filler	loud	playing	stayed	we're
defiling	finally	loneliest	proud	staying	what
deniable	fineness	loneliness	reacted	stoppable	what's
denied	finest	lonely	reclaimed	stopper	when
deny	fly	madden	refreshed	stopping	where
denying	flying	maddest	refusing	sturdier	whether
detract	friendliest	madness	relight	sturdiest	whole
did	friendliness	main	removal	sturdily	whose
driable	friendly	man	repressing	swimmer	widen
dried	gradable	matched	resounded	taking	wideness
drier	grader	misdeal	runner	they	widest
driest	grading	mismatching	running	they'll	woman
drily	happiest	misspell	sadden	thickest	womanly
drying	happily	movable	saddest	tract	worlds
duller	happiness	move	sadness	trappable	you've
edit	hated	nastier	she'll	trapper	

Section A

Bases introduced in Lessons 57–64

please	57	thought	58	count	59	grow	61
ease	57	fame	58	found	59	show	61
spray	57	glory	58	very	59	feat	61
straight	57	fury	58	ruin	61		
about	57	text	59	fluid	61		
hole	57	place	59	under	61		

Section B

Rules introduced in Lessons 57–64

Plural Variation (Lesson 57) "If a word ends in **consonant-and-y,** you add **es** to make the plural word."

Vowel-Consonant (Lesson 61) "If **w** is at the end of a morphograph, then it is a vowel letter."

Section C

Some words made of morphographs taught through Lesson 64

about	didn't	hopefulness	notion	running	unhappily
active	diner	hopeless	passage	sadder	unreal
arms	driest	hopelessly	passion	served	untried
babyish	dropping	hopelessness	place	shopping	usefully
barest	ease	hotly	planner	show	using
barred	exclaim	hotter	please	snapped	very
bars	expressive	hottest	portable	soundly	what's
bigger	facing	hurried	preserving	spray	widen
boxing	fact	hurrying	proclaimed	stays	widest
brotherly	fame	inactive	profiles	stepped	wonderfully
busily	fanciful	inhuman	profit	stopping	worked
buzzes	feat	leaving	profusely	straight	worldly
cares	filing	likable	proudly	straightened	worried
caring	fluid	likelihood	proverb	sturdier	
carriage	flying	lonelier	quietly	sturdiest	
cities	forceful	loneliest	raging	sturdily	
clannish	found	loudness	really	swimmer	
cloudiness	friendliness	madder	refinable	text	
coming	friendly	maddest	refined	they'll	
count	fury	madly	relatively	thought	
cried	fusion	manly	removal	thoughtful	
defaming	glory	mainly	renamed	thoughtfully	
deform	graded	mistaken	rental	thoughtfulness	
delightful	grow	misused	repression	thoughtless	
denies	hasn't	namable	reserved	thoughtlessly	
depart	hating	nastier	retraced	thoughtlessness	
depression	hole	nastiest	retraction	trial	
deserving	hopeful	nastily	rightfully	uncivil	
designer	hopefully	notable	ruin	under	

Appendix G

Section A

Bases introduced in Lessons 65–74

prove	65	side	66	pain	69	shape	71
poison	65	*ject*	66	brain	69	fry	71
blow	65	some	67	gain	69	physic	71
throw	65	out	67	sure	70	hero	72
cept	65	rich	67	cure	70	base	72
gress	65	sore	67	pure	70	prime	72
tect	65	shore	67	sent	70	tin	72
any	66	store	67	tent	70	spin	72
know	66	feet	67	graph	71	win	72
cause	66	give	69	phone	71	*tain*	72
pause	66	rain	69	photo	71		

Section B

Some words made from morphographs taught through Lesson 74

any
base
blow
blower
brain
catchy
cause
causing
cloudy
conception
contain
contented
cure
deceptive
detained
detective
easier
exception
famous
feet
finely
fineness
finest
fried
fry
furious
fuzzy
gain
gainfully

give
given
glorious
graph
happiest
happily
happiness
hero
incurable
injection
inside
know
knowing
lengthy
maddest
madly
madness
nightly
out
outside
pain
painfulness
pause
phone
photo
photograph
physic
physics
pleasure

poison
preside
pressure
prime
primed
procure
progression
progressive
project
protection
prove
pure
purely
rain
rainy
reception
refried
regain
regress
reinjected
resent
reside
restore
retain
retention
rich
riches
runny
sent

shape
shiniest
shiny
shore
side
snappy
some
sore
sorely
spin
spinning
store
sure
surely
tent
texture
throw
tin
undetectable
uninsured
unprotected
unproven
widely
wideness
widest
win
winner

Appendix H

Bases introduced in Lessons 75–83

quote	76	bet	77	state	78	first	81
quest	76	*pel*	77	spirit	79	thirst	81
quick	76	*vise*	78	chief	79	hop	81
quart	76	duty	78	niece	79	with	81
heavy	77	scope	78	grief	79	plant	81
breath	77	fail	78	brief	79	ship	81
head	77	rail	78	plain	80	tale	81
flat	77	tail	78	*duce*	80		

Section B

Some words made from morphographs taught through Lesson 83

activists
basics
bet
better
breath
breathlessness
brief
briefly
chief
chiefly
chiefs
conducive
conquest
consent
deduced
detail
devise
disclaims
discontented
discounted
discounts
disease
disliked
displace
displeasing
displeasure
disproves
disquieting
dispel

duties
duty
expel
explain
expressionist
fail
failure
first
flat
flatter
flatly
friendless
friendliness
glorious
gloriously
graphics
grief
head
headed
headless
heaviest
heavily
heavy
herbal
heroic
hop
hopelessness
hopped
hopping

induces
inquest
joyous
joyously
misquoting
misstated
motorist
nervous
nervously
niece
nieces
physical
physicist
plain
plainly
plant
planted
planting
plants
produce
producing
propel
provisions
quart
quarter
quest
question
questionable
quick

quicker
quickly
quotable
quote
rail
rails
realist
realistic
receptionist
reduce
reducing
reinstate
relativist
repel
request
requested
retail
retailer
revise
revision
scope
ship
shipped
shipping
spirit
spiritless
state
stately
station

stature
studious
studiously
tail
tailing
tale
thirst
thirstiness
thirsty
unheroic
unrealistic
unreduced
unrequested
unrevised
unstateliness
various
variously
vision
with
without

Section A

Bases introduced in Lessons 84–92

south	84	plane	85	get	88	cute	89
round	84	verse	85	road	88	athlete	89
cover	84	old	86	coat	88	muse	89
pound	84	hold	86	vote	88	magic	90
ground	84	bold	86	class	88	fashion	90
thousand	84	cold	86	sow	88	shake	90
danger	85	fold	86	cube	89	shed	90
chance	85	*fer*	86	huge	89	shout	90
		bid	88			*struct*	90

Section B

Rules introduced in Lessons 84–92

En Variation (Lesson 87) "When the word ends with the letter **w,** and you add **en,** drop the **e.**"

Section C

Some words made from morphographs taught through Lesson 92

athlete	cube	grounded	overthrown	shakiness	transporter
athletic	cubed	grown	plane	shaking	transporting
bid	cubic	hold	pound	shaky	unathletic
blown	cute	holding	poundage	shed	uncover
bold	cutest	huge	pounding	shedding	underground
boldness	danger	hugeness	prefer	shout	unfashionable
chance	dangerous	hugest	push	shown	unfold
chances	defer	infer	pushiness	south	unforgiving
chanciest	define	instruct	pushing	southerly	unfold
class	deform	instructing	pushy	sow	unknown
classes	depланed	instruction	railroad	sown	unshakable
classier	deserve	instructively	recovery	structure	unshaken
classy	destruction	inverse	refashioned	structuring	unstructured
coat	destructive	inversely	refer	thousand	verse
cold	detain	inversion	refine	thrown	version
coldest	discovered	known	reform	transacted	vote
coldly	fashion	magic	reserve	transaction	voter
confer	fashionable	magical	restructure	transactional	voting
confine	fashioned	magically	retain	transfer	withhold
conform	fold	muse	reversal	transformed	withholding
conserve	folder	music	reverse	transforming	
construct	forbid	musical	reversing	transfuse	
constructively	forget	musing	road	transfusing	
contain	forgive	old	round	transfusion	
converse	forgiven	olden	roundest	transgress	
conversely	forgiveness	oldest	sew	transgression	
conversion	get	outclassed	sewn	transplant	
cover	getting	overcoats	shake	transplanted	
covering	ground	overgrown	shakes	transport	

Bases introduced in Lessons 93–106

logic	93	tend	95	live	96	sweet	98	bug	99
part	93	type	95	life	96	shelf	98	range	100
settle	93	pose	95	fore	96	sun	98	month	100
little	93	train	95	choose	97	*cur*	98	long	100
ample	93	faint	95	loose	97	star	99	came	100
middle	93	wife	95	soon	97	rob	99	scribe	100
four	93	loaf	95	cool	97	dim	99	love	100
leaf	94	son	95	room	97	bed	99	join	101
half	94	*fect*	96	broom	97	hid	99	oil	101
thief	94	reach	96	govern	98	leg	99	spoil	101
wolf	94	speak	96	cross	98	mud	99	major	101
calf	94	reason	96	speech	98	grab	99	test	101
self	94	court	96	sleep	98	blot	99	*mit*	101

Rules introduced in Lessons 93–106

Al Insertion (Lesson 95) "When the word ends in the letters **ic,** you must add the morphograph **al** before adding **ly.**"

Plural Variation (Lesson 101) "Some words that end in the sound **fff** have the letters **ves** in the plural. You can always hear the sound **vvv** in the plural."

Section C

Some words made from morphographs taught through Lesson 106

across	compartment	dejected	injected	magically	perfect	room	thief
actual	compass	dejection	instruction	major	performer	roomy	thieves
again	compassion	departure	intended	manhood	permit	scribe	train
ahead	compel	describe	intent	middle	pertaining	self	training
alike	composer	dimness	intention	misspell	physically	selfless	transmit
alive	compound	dispel	join	month	pose	settle	transpose
alone	compression	example	joined	motherhood	pretending	settlement	type
ample	conceptual	exposure	leaf	mouth	project	shelf	typically
amused	concur	expression	leaves	movement	projected	shelves	unlovable
amusement	confection	extending	life	musically	projection	shipment	unreachable
apartment	confinement	factually	lifelessness	object	range	sleep	unrealistic
around	conjoin	faint	little	objected	reach	son	unselfish
aside	consignment	fainted	littlest	objection	reached	soon	unsettling
basically	container	fore	live	objectively	realistically	sooner	unusual
boyhood	contended	four	livelihood	oblong	reason	speak	usually
breathtaking	context	govern	living	observable	recur	speaker	visually
broom	contextual	government	loaf	obstruction	rejoined	speech	wife
calf	cool	grabby	logic	obtained	remit	spoil	wives
calves	court	gradually	logically	oil	repel	spoiled	wolf
came	cross	graphically	long	ourselves	repose	statement	wolves
choose	decompress	half	loose	part	respell	sun	yourself
choosy	defect	heroically	loosened	parties	retyped	sweet	yourselves
classically	defectiveness	induced	love	partly	robber	tend	
commitment	deject	inject	loveliest	perception	robbery	test	

Appendix K

Section A

Bases introduced in Lessons 107–112

merge	107	frog	107	family	108	shave	109
verge	107	trip	107	drive	108	knife	109
dress	107	ton	107	while	108	strain	109
just	107	gun	107	double	108	puff	109
critic	107	net	107	couple	108	gulf	109
vent	107	pig	107	trouble	108	*vert*	109
hit	107	rat	107	*sist*	108		
spot	107	chin	107	pretty	109		

Section B

Some words made from morphographs taught through Lesson 112

alongside	critically	improve	persist	subsist
aloud	decomposable	improvement	physically	subtract
amusement	decompression	impure	portion	thieves
arise	defective	incur	prettily	thoughtlessly
asleep	deserving	indescribably	pretty	transport
athletically	desist	insisted	prevent	trouble
atypically	detainment	intention	proportion	troublesome
author	double	invent	puff	unimpressed
aversive	doubly	invention	puffiness	unimproved
became	dress	inverse	quarterly	unjustly
because	dressers	inverted	quietness	unknown
becoming	dressiness	just	reasoning	unquestionable
before	drive	knife	reception	unshaven
befriend	driver	knives	relive	unspeakable
behave	emit	lengthen	resisted	unreachable
beheaded	equally	lifelong	restraining	unusually
belittle	exposed	liveliness	reversal	vent
belonging	factual	loaves	reverted	verge
beloved	families	logically	selfishly	whether
calves	family	magically	share	while
carrier	governing	merge	shave	wives
civilly	gradual	merger	shelves	wolfish
compound	grandson	misbehaved	statement	wolves
conceptual	graphically	musically	straightened	yourself
consist	gulf	nervous	strain	yourselves
constrained	gulfs	objection	strengthen	
content	halves	observer	sturdiness	
convention	heroically	obstructively	subhuman	
converge	impel	obtained	subject	
conversion	imported	overdrive	subjective	
converted	impose	overextended	submerge	
coolly	impounded	perceptive	submit	
couple	impressionable	perfectly	subscriber	
critic	impressively	perform	subside	

Appendix L

Section A

Bases introduced in Lessons 113–123

hog	113	solve	113	add	116	screen	119	cap	122
gas	113	week	113	sect	116	freeze	119	up	122
car	113	ply	114	stance	116	*dict*	119	fog	122
pan	113	build	114	*sume*	116	*cise*	120	pop	122
bud	113	lake	114	watch	117	*fess*	120	bat	122
top	113	script	114	science	117	*ceed*	120	stir	122
gum	113	*ceive*	114	view	117	ready	121	tip	122
cut	113	bought	115	circle	117	point	121	sit	122
red	113	fought	115	*lent*	117	beauty	121	dig	122
body	113	ought	115	*plete*	117	over	121		
wise	113	brought	115	*plore*	117	value	121		
puzzle	113	day	115	mote	118	marry	121		
table	113	weak	115	speed	119	set	122		

Section B

Rules introduced in Lessons 113–123

Doubling Rule (Lesson 113) "When the word ends in a short **cvc** morphograph, use the doubling rule."

O-r Ending (Lesson 118) "Use **o-r** if a form of the word ends in **i-o-n**."

Section C

Some words made from morphographs taught through Lesson 123

add	bought	decision	emotionless	inferring	precision	repress	supposed
addict	brought	decisive	exploration	information	predictable	repression	surface
addiction	build	demote	explore	inscription	prediction	repressive	surname
address	building	deplete	express	insect	preview	resolved	surrounded
adjust	circle	deplorable	expression	instance	primate	restoration	table
adjustment	circling	depress	expressive	invaluable	proceed	resume	tentative
adventure	commotion	depression	faction	lake	professional	reviewer	thieves
adventurer	complete	description	factor	leaves	professor	revision	tractor
adverb	completely	designation	factory	marriage	promoted	science	unadvised
adversely	completion	detector	formation	marry	promotion	screen	uneventful
advise	complying	devaluation	fought	motion	protector	script	unrelenting
applied	compressor	dictation	freeze	motivate	puzzle	scriptural	unsupported
attainable	conceivable	dictatorship	freezer	notation	puzzling	sect	valuable
attend	conciseness	diction	friendship	objector	quotation	sections	value
attention	condense	digress	graduation	ought	readiness	setting	view
attested	confess	discovered	halves	over	ready	solve	visor
attraction	confessor	dissect	imploring	overcoat	received	speed	watch
attractive	connotative	dissolved	implying	overreacted	referring	speeding	weak
authorship	conscience	distance	impress	overview	relent	stance	weakness
beautiful	consume	edict	impression	plantation	relentless	substances	week
beauty	consumer	eject	impressive	ply	remote	supplant	weekly
bodies	conversation	emerge	inattentively	point	repelled	supply	wise
bodily	day	emitted	incision	pointed	replied	supportive	wisest
body	deceived	emotion	incomplete	precisely	reply	suppose	wolves

Section A

Bases introduced in Lessons 124–140

merry	124	super	128	medic	131	stood	134
spire	124	mend	128	after	131	*pute*	134
sane	124	cave	128	break	131	ever	135
post	124	there	129	*mise*	131	nine	135
miss	124	scarce	130	*clude*	132	seven	135
cord	124	ideal	130	*vide*	132	*quire*	135
tour	125	grave	130	*gin*	132	got	135
dense	125	duct	130	air	133	sire	135
simple	125	*stant*	130	birth	133	*soci*	136
their	126	pare	130	ball	133	collar	136
cess	126	*trol*	130	noon	133	image	136
cern	126	*lect*	131	*pense*	133	*hilar*	136
rect	126	*turb*	131	teen	134		
tense	128	date	131	stand	134		

Section B

Some words made from morphographs taught through Lesson 140

according	compromise	disreputable	ideally	logician	preparing	scarcely	teen
accordion	computation	disturb	image	magician	pretense	scarcity	tense
acquire	computer	divide	imagination	majority	prevent	secluded	tenseness
actor	concave	downward	imagine	medic	preventable	secure	tension
admission	conclude	duct	include	medically	prevention	security	their
after	conductor	election	indict	medicine	procession	select	there
afternoon	conferred	elective	indirectly	mend	product	selective	tour
air	conspired	equalize	individual	merry	production	service	tourism
airport	contour	ever	inexpensive	miss	productivity	seven	tourists
amend	control	every	inquire	motorized	promise	seventeen	transferred
amendment	controller	excess	inquiry	musician	propeller	sideward	unable
aspiring	cord	excessively	insane	nine	provided	simple	unamended
authorized	criticism	excluding	insanity	nineteen	realism	simply	unbreakable
backward	criticize	exhilarate	insecurity	noon	realize	sociable	uncivilized
ball	date	expense	inspirational	notice	recapped	social	uncontrolled
beginning	deduction	expensive	inspired	permission	recess	spiraling	understand
birth	dense	expensively	instantly	perspire	recession	spire	understood
birthdate	desirable	facial	intensively	perturbed	recommend	spiritual	undesirable
break	desire	forbidden	intercepted	physician	record	stand	undisturbed
breaking	detour	forgot	interjection	post	recorder	standing	unmanned
cave	dictate	forgotten	intermission	postage	referred	stood	unnoticed
cavity	dictation	forward	intersect	poster	repelled	submitted	unplanned
civilian	dictator	fourteen	interview	postscript	reputable	substantial	unprepared
collar	diction	got	introduce	precludes	reputation	super	unrecorded
commission	direct	grave	introduction	predict	required	superhuman	unsnapped
committed	direction	gravity	invent	predictable	requirement	superimpose	upwardly
comparably	discern	hilarity	invention	prediction	sane	supervise	verbalize
compare	dispenser	humanity	inventor	preferred	sanitation	supervision	visualize
compelled	disputed	ideal	justice	prepare	scarce	surrealism	withstand

Meanings of Nonword Bases, Prefixes, Suffixes

Starred morphographs (*) may function either as words or as nonword bases.

Morphograph	Lesson	Meanings	Examples
a-	95	(in, on, at; not, without)	ahead; apart, atypical
-able	10	(can be)	stretchable, washable, readable
ac-	125	(to, toward)	accept, account, access
ad-	114	(to, toward, against)	advise, adjustment, admitted
-age	28	(that which is; state)	usage, package, marriage
-al	30	(related to, like)	formal, structural, trial
ap-	124	(to, toward, against)	appointment, approval, appendage
at-	119	(to, toward, against)	attract, attention, attest
-ate	122	(to make, act; having the quality of)	evaluate, activate; passionate
be-	107	(really; by, over; to make)	became; beside; because
ceed	120	(to go)	proceed, exceedingly, succeed
ceive	114	(to take; contain)	receiver, conceive; deceived
cent*	17	(hundred[th])	percentage, century
cept	65	(to take, contain)	receptive, intercept, acceptable
cern	126	(separate)	concern, discerning
cess	126	(to go)	process, excessive, recession
cise	120	(to cut)	incision, concise, precisely
clude	132	(to close)	include, excluded, concluding
com-	97	(with, together)	compress, combat, commission
con-	40	(with, together)	conform, contest, condense
cord*	124	(heart)	record, accord, cordial
cur	98	(to run, to happen)	concur, recurred, current
cure*	70	(to heal, to care for)	curator, secure, inaccurate
de-	24	(away from, down)	deport, depend, describe
di-	120	(through, across; twice)	divert, direct; divide
dict	119	(to speak; to fix)	diction; predict
dis-	75	(opposite of, not)	dispel, discount, disease
duce	80	(to lead)	produce, educate, reducing
duct*	130	(to lead)	productive, conductor, deduction
e-	112	(out, away)	eject, event, emitted
-ed	15	(in the past)	stepped, cried, formed

-en	27	(to make)	loosen, proven, golden
-er	18	(more; one who)	easier, lighter; boxer
-es	38	(more than one, a verb marker for **he, she,** or **it**)	matches, boxes, carries
-est	4	(the most)	lightest, happiest, friendliest
ex-	53	(out, away)	export, exclude, extend
fact*	53	(to make)	factual, factory, factor
fect	96	(to do, to make)	defective, confection, perfect
fer	86	(to carry)	transfer, infer, referred
fess	120	(to speak)	profess, confession, professor
fine*	14	(the end)	finest, final, infinite
fit*	41	(to suit)	outfit, profit, benefit
for-	89	(against, completely)	forbid, forgotten, forgiving
found*	59	(to base, to establish)	profound, founder, foundation
-ful	25	(full of; tending to)	careful, beautiful; forgetful
fuse*	37	(to pour or melt)	refuse, transfusion, confused
graph*	71	(chart; to write)	photograph; graphite
gress	65	(to step)	regression, progress, transgression
hilar	136	(merry)	exhilarate, hilarity, hilarious
-hood	100	(state, quality)	motherhood, likelihood, childhood
-ial	124	(related to, like)	partial, facial, adverbial
-ian	126	(one who)	magician, musician, civilian
-ic	80	(like, related to)	basic, typically, artistic
-ice	129	(act of; time of)	justice; service, notice
im-	108	(in, into; not)	impose, impression; impurity
in-	39	(in, into; not; really)	include; incurable; invaluable
-ine	133	(related to; feminine)	medicine, imagine; heroine
-ing	1	(when you do something)	spending, moving, stopping
inter-	128	(between)	interact, intersect, intervention
intro-	127	(inside)	introduce, introvert, introduction
-ion	61	(state, quality, act or process)	action, taxation, repression
-ish	31	(inclined)	childish, selfish, stylish
-ism	131	(state, quality)	tourism, criticism, realism
-ist	77	(one who)	artist, typist, tourist
-ite	126	(related)	composite, definite, cavity
-ive	59	(one who; quality of)	relative; expressive, informative

-ize	132	(to make more)	humanize, civilize, formalize
ject	66	(to throw)	rejecting, dejected, projection
late*	41	(to carry; wide)	translate, relation; dilate
lect	131	(to gather)	select, elect, lecture
-less	6	(without)	painless, useless, restlessness
-ly	19	(how something is done)	equally, basically, quietly
main*	53	(to stay)	mainland, remain
mend*	128	(fault)	amendment, commendable, recommendation
-ment	94	(result of doing something)	placement, requirement, apartment
merge*	107	(plunge)	merger, emerge, submerge
mis-	7	(wrongly)	misspell, mistrial, misprint
mise	131	(to send)	demise, premise, promise
miss*	124	(to send)	admission, dismiss, missile
mit	101	(to send)	transmit, admitted, commitment
mote	118	(to move)	motionless, demote, promotional
muse*	89	(one of the nine Muses)	amusement, bemused, musical
-ness	9	(that which is; quality)	thoughtfulness; thickness, uselessness
ob-	93	(to, toward, against)	obstruct, obtain; objection
-or	118	(one who; that which)	instructor, actor; factor
-ous	67	(having the quality of)	famous, furious, joyous
pare*	130	(equal)	preparing, separate, compare
pass*	27	(to suffer)	passive, impassioned
pel	77	(to push)	expel, propeller, repellent
pense	133	(to pay)	expense, compensate, pension
per-	96	(through)	perform, pertain, perceive
plain*	80	(flat; to lament)	explainable; complain, plaintive
plete	117	(full)	incomplete, deplete, repletion
plore	117	(to cry)	explore, implore, deplorable
ply*	114	(a layer, to fold; full)	pliable; comply, supplier
port*	4	(to carry)	import, transportation, portable
pose*	95	(to act a certain way; to put, to place)	composure, opposite; position
pound*	84	(to place)	compound, expound
pre-	16	(before)	preview, preclude, predict
pro-	57	(in favor of; before; foward)	proclaim; provision; progress

prove*	65	(useful)	approval, improvement
pute	134	(to reckon)	computer, dispute, reputation
quest*	76	(to seek, to ask for)	conquest, request, questionable
quire	135	(to seek, to ask for)	acquire, required, inquiring
re-	1	(again, back)	rerun, return, repack
rect	126	(straight)	direct, resurrect, correct
-s	36	(more than one, a verb marker for **he, she,** or **it**)	parks, friends, designs
sane*	124	(healthy)	insane, sanitation, unsanitary
scribe*	100	(to write)	describe, prescribe, subscriber
script*	114	(to write)	descriptive, prescription, subscript
se-	133	(apart)	secluded, inseparable, selection
sect*	116	(to cut)	section, dissect, intersect
sent*	70	(to feel)	resentment, consent, dissent
serve*	16	(to save)	preserve, conservative
-ship	116	(state, quality)	friendship, hardship, relationship
side*	66	(to sit)	preside, residual
sist	108	(to stand, to set; to make)	persist, resist; consist
soci	136	(companion)	sociable, association, socialize
sort*	4	(to go out)	assortment, consort, resort
spire*	124	(breath)	respiration, inspiring
stance*	116	(to stand, to set)	instance, substance, distance
stant	130	(to stand, to set)	constant, substantial, instant
struct	90	(to build)	structure, destruction, constructive
sub-	109	(under)	subtract, subhuman, submission
sume	116	(to take)	consumer, resume, presumably
sup-	117	(under)	support, suppressed, supposed
sur-	117	(under; over, above)	submarine; surname, surpass, surround
tail*	78	(to cut)	detailed, retail, tailor
tain	72	(to hold)	retaining, container, detained
tect	65	(to cover)	detecting, protection
tend*	95	(to be inclined to; to stretch)	attend, intend; extend
tent*	70	(to stretch)	retention, content, intently
text*	59	(to weave)	textile, context, texture
tour*	125	(to turn)	detour, contour
tract*	53	(to drag; to draw)	subtraction; tractor, attractive

trans-	85	(across)	transportation, transform, transfer
trol	130	(regulate)	controller
turb	131	(to agitate)	perturb, disturb, turbulent
-ual	99	(related to, like)	factual, usual, gradual
un-	3	(not, reversal of)	unhappy, unusual, untie
-ure	65	(state)	departure, pressure, failure
vent*	107	(an outlet, to come)	prevent, invention, adventure
verge*	107	(to lean)	converge, diverge
verse*	85	(to turn)	conversation, reversal, versatile
vert	109	(to turn)	invert, convert, introvert
vide	132	(to see; to separate)	providing; divide, individual
vise*	78	(to see; to separate)	advise, visual; division
-ward	133	(toward)	backward, homeward, outwardly
-y	70	(having the quality of)	shiny, activity, doggy

Five-Lesson Point Summaries

	Lesson	1	2	3	4	5	Total
1.	Points						

	Lesson	6	7	8	9	10	Total
2.	Points						

	Lesson	11	12	13	14	15	Total
3.	Points						

	Lesson	16	17	18	19	20	Total
4.	Points						

	Lesson	21	22	23	24	25	Total
5.	Points						

	Lesson	26	27	28	29	30	Total
6.	Points						

	Lesson	31	32	33	34	35	Total
7.	Points						

	Lesson	36	37	38	39	40	Total
8.	Points						

	Lesson	41	42	43	44	45	Total
9.	Points						

	Lesson	46	47	48	49	50	Total
10.	Points						

	Lesson	51	52	53	54	55	Total
11.	Points						

	Lesson	56	57	58	59	60	Total
12.	Points						

	Lesson	61	62	63	64	65	Total
13.	Points						

	Lesson	66	67	68	69	70	Total
14.	Points						

Five-Lesson Point Summaries

	Lesson	71	72	73	74	75	Total
15.	Points						

	Lesson	76	77	78	79	80	Total
16.	Points						

	Lesson	81	82	83	84	85	Total
17.	Points						

	Lesson	86	87	88	89	90	Total
18.	Points						

	Lesson	91	92	93	94	95	Total
19.	Points						

	Lesson	96	97	98	99	100	Total
20.	Points						

	Lesson	101	102	103	104	105	Total
21.	Points						

	Lesson	106	107	108	109	110	Total
22.	Points						

	Lesson	111	112	113	114	115	Total
23.	Points						

	Lesson	116	117	118	119	120	Total
24.	Points						

	Lesson	121	122	123	124	125	Total
25.	Points						

	Lesson	126	127	128	129	130	Total
26.	Points						

	Lesson	131	132	133	134	135	Total
27.	Points						

	Lesson	136	137	138	139	140	Total
28.	Points						

Five-Lesson Point Summary Graph

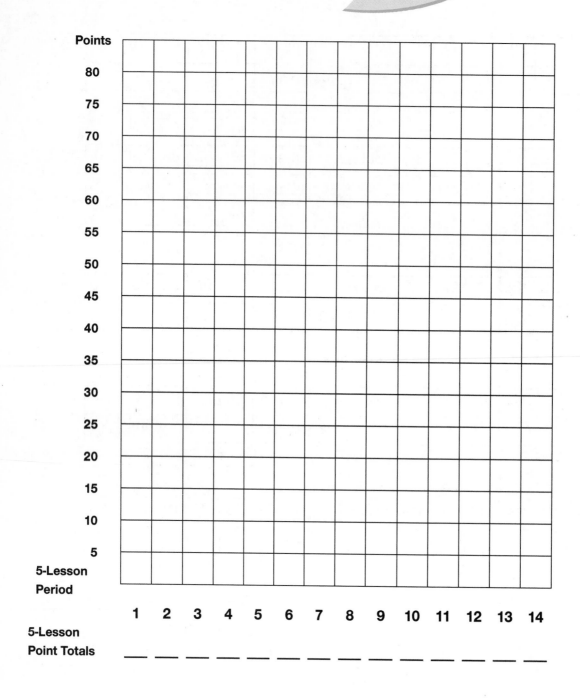

Points

80
75
70
65
60
55
50
45
40
35
30
25
20
15
10
5

5-Lesson Period

1　2　3　4　5　6　7　8　9　10　11　12　13　14

5-Lesson Point Totals

__ __ __ __ __ __ __ __ __ __ __ __ __ __

Five-Lesson Point Summary Graph

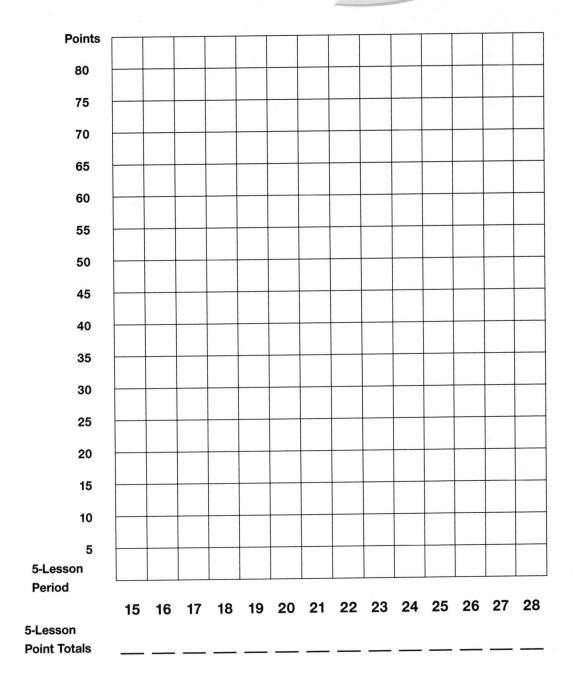

Points

| 80 |
| 75 |
| 70 |
| 65 |
| 60 |
| 55 |
| 50 |
| 45 |
| 40 |
| 35 |
| 30 |
| 25 |
| 20 |
| 15 |
| 10 |
| 5 |

5-Lesson Period

15 16 17 18 19 20 21 22 23 24 25 26 27 28

5-Lesson Point Totals

___ ___ ___ ___ ___ ___ ___ ___ ___ ___ ___ ___ ___ ___

FOR THE STUDENT:

I want to become a better speller. I agree to work hard and follow the teacher's instructions. I understand that my grade will be determined on the following basis:

A Grade—If the average of my five-lesson totals is at least 55 points.

B Grade—If the average of my five-lesson totals is 45 to 54 points.

C Grade—If the average of my five-lesson totals is 35 to 44 points.

I understand that an average of less than 35 points per five lessons is a failing grade for this course.

Daily points will be awarded by the teacher as follows:

1. Oral work   0–3 group points for working hard and answering on signal. Everyone in the group will receive the same number of points for oral work each day.

2. Bonus   0–4 points that can be earned from time to time for special work that will be explained by the teacher.

3. Worksheet

Errors	Points
0–2	10
3	7
4	5
5	3
6	1
7 or more	0

4. Corrections: I will lose 3 points every time I do not correct a worksheet error.

I will total my daily points every five lessons.

FOR THE TEACHER:

I want my students to become better spellers. I agree to work hard preparing every lesson and to teach to the best of my abilities. I will award points and grades according to the terms of this contract.

_____   _____
Student   *Teacher*